THE RADIO KENT GARDENERS' GUIDE

BY HARRY SMITH & BOB COLLARD

CARTOONS BY KEATON

MERESBOROUGH BOOKS
1989

Published by Meresborough Books, 17 Station Road, Rainham, Kent. ME8 7RS in association with BBC Radio Kent.

Meresborough Books is a specialist publisher of books about Kent. A list of titles currently in print will be found at the back of this book.

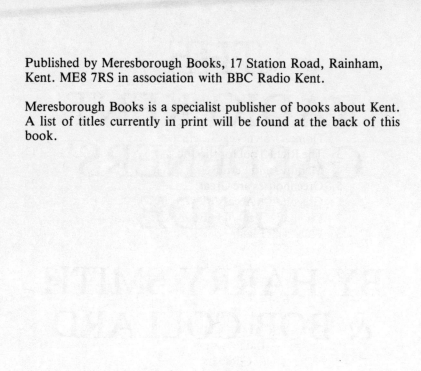

ISBN 0948193 45 X

Printed by Mackays of Chatham plc.

Contents

3

Foreword

Lucky indeed are the gardeners of Kent, for they live in the Garden of England. For many years it has been our privilege to meet many of them, visit their gardens, hear of their problems and learn their crafty ways of dealing with tricky jobs. From them this modest book has been born, and to them it is dedicated.

Harry Smith and Bob Collard

'My soil test says it's clay.'

Chapter One

The Answer Lies in the Kentish Soil

Few counties in England have such a range of different soils as Kent.
— Just listen at any horticultural society! From chalk in the north,
through Wealden clay and Greensand beds, the layers of underlying
rocks have, through millions of years, produced quite different top-
soils, sometimes varying from street to street or even within a garden
plot. Each kind of soil has its good points and offers challenges too.
But with patience over the years, good results can be gained almost
anywhere — given time.

Gardening on chalk
Right along the North Downs, from Dartford to Dover, the solid
chalk is covered with a topsoil layer sometimes only a few inches
thick, and its alkaline nature makes the growing of lime-hating
plants like rhododendrons and some heathers a terrible waste of
time. Such soils are quick to drain and soon suffer in really dry
spells, but can be greatly improved if plenty of manure or compost is
worked in over the years to give water-retaining humus and
improved fertility. The secret is to concentrate on the kinds of plant
that thrive in chalky ground, and look around the area to see which
plants are doing well.

Succeeding on sand
Light sandy soils are the gardener's favourite for easy digging. The
rapid drainage means the plot can be worked soon after heavy rain,
but it also allows those plant foods in the soil to be washed or
'leached' away. Again the secret is humus: that rotted-down vege-
tation which soaks up water like a sponge and helps hold vital plant
food ready for their roots. Most sandy soils have a low pH, and
while this acidity suits certain plants, many vegetables for instance
will benefit from the ground being limed from time to time as
mentioned later on.

Coping with clay
Heavy to work and slow to drain when wet, soils in the clayey parts
of Kent give surely the greatest challenge of all! (And often the best
of excuses!) A brand-new garden on thick clay can be a discouraging
place indeed, but each year's cultivation brings easier working.

Large amounts of coarse, sharp sand can improve the drainage enormously if worked well in, and organic matter again works wonders with clay in time. It is the longest and hardest kind of soil to lick into shape, but one which responds with a wealth of happy plants in the end. Also, a garden on clay is usually the last to show signs of distress in drought, as well as being less liable to leaching. Liming (but not at the same time as manure!) can also help assist with drainage to some extent, as it tends to cause the clay's microscopic particles to join and form slightly larger lumps. Frost can also play a useful part in breaking down clay soils if the ground is dug 'rough' and left in largish lumps on the surface.

Testing the soil
Whatever kind of ground your garden has, regular testing will help a lot by making sure the soil has enough nutrients and is the right pH for the plants to be grown there. Several kinds of simple testing kits are available, and these work with chemical indicators which change colour to compare with a chart. The main plant foods can be checked, as well as the all-important pH. This is a measure of the soil's acidity or alkalinity, and ranges from about pH4.5 (very acid), to pH7.5 (alkaline). Neutral is pH7 and most plants are happiest on just the acid side of neutral. The samples needed for soil testing are very small, and several should be taken across the plot to ensure reliable results.

Chapter Two

Planning and planting the plot for home-grown veg

Vegetables can play a tasty part in any garden scheme, but only grow the kinds you like! Start by making a simple plan (squared paper helps) to show where each row of seeds or planting is to go. This can be done well beforehand, and gives a chance to order what is wanted. At the same time, bear in mind that different kinds of crop such as brassicas (cabbages, cauliflowers etc), root crops and peas and beans have various manurial requirements (or none at all), so certain kinds are usually kept together in part of a plot, and others grown elsewhere. In following years, they are moved to another part. This 'rotation' also helps to prevent an accumulation of pests and diseases associated with certain kinds of crop. Many reference books give plans for planting, but always adapt them to suit your needs.

Preparing the ground
Ideally, all perennial weeds such as ground elder, bell-bine and horsetail should be killed and removed the year beforehand, and if time can be spared and the backache suffered, the final results will be worth it. Many weeds respond to chemical treatment, but some such as horsetail are best eliminated by covering the ground with black polythene for a year. This need not prove quite so unsightly as it sounds, as successful temporary crops like potatoes can be planted to grow up through cross-type openings cut in the sheet, and thus help clean the ground.

On really heavy soils such as our Kentish Wealden clay, cultivation of the weed-free plot should start in autumn by digging the ground roughly and leaving in largish lumps. Winter frost will break them down and help create a good 'tilth' for sowing and planting. On lighter soils this can also provide good exercise, but may be just as well left until spring unless manure needs working in. This should be done early so it breaks down well, but only do it for certain crops. If roots such as carrots and parsnips are grown on freshly-manured ground, they tend to form forked or 'sproggy' roots which are unsightly and amazingly hard to prepare for the pot.

Brassicas thrive on well-manured ground, and also appreciate lime if acid conditions prevail. But never add lime at the same time as manure or ammonia may be released.

'A bit sticky to sow yet Sid.'

Getting ready for sowing

Never start sowing seeds until the soil is right; remember our old gardeners' maxim; walk across the plot; if soil sticks to your boots the ground is too wet. Wait a while. Start by lightly forking the ground, tread it gently, and then rake along the row to prepare a suitable seed bed with a tilth like breadcrumbs. Sowing depth depends on the size of seed, and instructions on the packet should be followed (or see our guide below). Use a tight garden line to ensure a straight row, keep one foot on it to hold it steady, and use a corner of the draw hoe to take out the right depth of drill. Cover the seeds carefully with the back of the rake, and firm down gently with it held flat. Always mark the ends of each row with a label written with soft lead pencil which doesn't fade in the sun or rain. Please do not label with the packet on a stick! A few radish seeds at each end of the row are also a useful marker as they germinate quickly. Larger seeds like peas are best sown in a drill about four inches wide, and either scattered along it, or neatly spaced out if preferred and patience permits. Galvanized wire-netting pea guards are useful to protect the tender plants in their early stages, but remove them before the tendrils gain a grip. Mice can sometimes be a problem, and one old remedy was to treat the peas beforehand with paraffin and red lead. Gorse or holly clippings have sometimes been found effective too.

Potatoes are number one!

The fine flavour of freshly dug new potatoes keeps them a firm favourite with most gardeners, and the cultivation needed makes them a useful crop for cleaning ground. Choose early varieties and, several weeks before planting time, set the tubers in trays so their eyes can see the light, to start sprouting or 'chitting'. This needs doing in a light, airy, frost-proof place and gives a better yield of larger spuds at harvest time.

Lazy gardeners sometimes use a dibber to plant potatoes, but it is far better in Kent to take out a furrow with a Canterbury hoe and set the tubers a foot apart on a bed of well-rotted garden compost.

Earth up well over the row to protect from frost, light and any blight spores washed down by the rain. Given good conditions, the first tasty crop should be ready for digging in twelve weeks' time, but only lift them as needed as they retain their first-class fresh flavour and have time to grow. Many different varieties are available each year so try a few to see which you prefer. Foremost is a good early one, as are Vanessa and Cara.

Runner beans

Just as freshly dug new potatoes have a taste that is all their own, the flavour of freshly-picked runner beans is worth waiting many months to savour! They are also one of the most trouble-free garden vegetables we know, and give a splendid crop as long as a few simple points are followed.

Preparing the ground

Runner bean plants make most of their growth at the driest time of year, so the ground where they grow must be able to retain lots of water for these thirsty plants. Some time during winter or early spring, take out a trench at least a foot wide and two feet deep (or thereabouts), and put in as much bulky organic matter as can be spared, mixing it in layers with the soil as you put it back. Tread the trench at intervals, and try to leave the finished level slightly below the surrounding ground. The trench can then be left until planting time. Tall runner beans tend to shade other crops on the plot, so they are best kept at one end where this will not happen. Ours have been on the same spot for twenty years and still give splendid results!

Choosing the seed

Old gardeners used to save their own runner bean seed from year to year; and if properly ripened and stored this works well. But most of us have to rely on buying a packet of seed — and the choice is a wide one. In recent years, stringless runner beans have been developed, and these can save much fiddly work when preparing the beans for the pot.

Supporting the crop

The traditional Kentish way of supporting runner beans was by using chestnut poles or thick 'hop string'. Chestnut poles are now a bit hard to come by, and strings can tend to weave about in high winds. Tall bamboo canes are the favourite for most gardeners, and can be fixed to wires stretched between stout poles or stakes at each end of the trench. A single row of canes can be used, or a double row tied together at the top and pushed in at the bottom along both sides of the trench.

Sowing the seed

The beans can be put in the soil at the growing positions in May, but for the earliest and best crops, we always sow ours in the frost-free greenhouse the previous month and plant them out in mid-May. The wooden 'Dutch trays' tomatoes come in are ideal for this sowing of beans, and can be saved in the shed from year to year. Fill them with good compost (we use our own sifted garden compost with excellent results), and space the beans two inches apart each way on the

12

surface. Then poke them about an inch below compost level and 'scrabble' the surface to cover them. The labelled trays can then be laid under the greenhouse staging until the welcome shoots appear. Then put in full light and keep watered. Once the young beans are about two inches high, put the trays in the cold frame to harden off, and remember to close the frame lights at night if frost is forecast.

Planting out
Around Chelsea Show time, use a stout trowel to set out a plant on each side of the supporting cane or pole, firm in with the fingers, and water well to settle the roots. If the growing plants seem disinclined to climb, give them a helping hand by winding the wavering shoots (clockwise remember!) and tying with soft twine.

If the roots are kept moist, you will have little trouble in getting the flowers to 'set', but two old tricks are spraying with tepid water in the morning, or syringing the rows with a weak solution of lime in water.

Keep the beans well watered in dry spells, and give a liquid feed every few days. Once the young beans are large enough, be sure to pick regularly to keep further pods coming along. Once they are allowed to dry and ripen, the crop will tail off. When the season finally finishes, leave the old roots in the ground to give added nitrogen — or save a couple of roots to plant in the frost-free greenhouse for some really early beans next year!

Know your onions!
Some of the biggest and best onions in the country are grown in Kent, and although these showbench monsters may not be your cup of tea, there are few families where a good supply of such valuable veg will not come amiss. By far the simplest way to grow some very passable onions is to use 'sets' — those tiny bulbs the seedsmen sell in spring. Planted on well-manured ground and protected from the tweaking beaks of playful birds, these can give a crop as good as anything sold in the shops. With a frost-free greenhouse and propagator, raising onions from seed is far cheaper, and offers even larger bulbs at harvest time. For prize-winning specimens choose seeds of Kelsae or Robinson's Mammoth, and sow an inch apart each way in small trays of compost. Boxing Day is when the top growers do it, and the seedlings are potted on, hardened-off, and planted out in April – May on that all-important well-manured piece of ground. Keep onion crops weeded well and there is little else to do except to watch them grow. Careful harvesting when ready is the secret of long-keeping bulbs, and they are best allowed to dry off on

wire-netting frames in the greenhouse before storing in trays or 'strings' in a cool but dry and frost-free place.

The third, and simplest, way of growing your onions is to sow them in drills in the spring just like most other veg. Thinning as they grow is vital and gives lots of 'spring onions' for those summer salads. If kept well watered and weeded, some pretty passable onions can be gathered at harvest time and all for the price of a packet of seed.

Asparagus

Finally, and for sheer luxury from the vegetable plot if there is space to spare, an established asparagus bed can give a succulent but all-too-short crop of this King of Vegetables, in return for quite a small amount of work in later years. As always, preparation pays dividends, and a bed of rich ground must be achieved by working in as much well-rotted manure as possible, to at least a spade's depth. The best asparagus is grown from 'crowns' which are young plants one or two years old, and these are planted in April in shallow trenches on the bed and spaced a foot apart each way. When their roots have been spread as widely as possible, they are covered with four inches of soil and the crop left uncut in the first season after planting. Only a few of the succulent spears should be cut in the following year, and even in succeeding years all cutting should cease by the end of June. The remaining shoots are allowed to grow supported by canes and build up the roots, and cut back to ground level once the growth turns yellow in late October. A mulch of well-rotted manure several inches deep should be spread over the bed in late January, and it should be kept as free of weeds as possible throughout the year. Seedlings from the asparagus plants themselves were once a nuisance, but today's all-male strains like Lucullus have made these 'volunteers' a thing of the past.

Sowing spacings for super veg — all seeds thinly sown!
Beetroot. In rows 15″ apart and 1″ deep.
Brassicas. Sow ¾″ deep in prepared seed bed and transplant later.
Broad Beans. 3″ deep and 9″ apart in double (9″ apart) row.
Carrots. ¾″ deep in rows 9 – 12″ apart.
Dwarf French Beans. 2″ deep 6″ apart in rows 1′ apart.
Lettuce. ½″ deep and thin to 9 – 12″ apart. Rows 1′ apart.
Onion (seed). ½″ deep in rows 9″ apart. Thin to 3″ then 6″.
Onion (sets). Plant just covered 6 – 9″ apart. Rows 1′ apart.
Parsley. In rows ½″ deep and 6″ apart. Thin plants to 6″ apart.
Parsnip. ½″ deep in rows 12 – 15″ apart. Thin plants to 6 – 8″ apart.
Peas. Space at 2″ in three rows in 4″ wide drill 2″ deep.
Potatoes. Set tubers 1′ apart in rows 2′6″ apart.

Radish. ¼ – ½ʺ deep in rows 6ʺ apart.
Runner Beans. 2 – 3ʺ deep and 6ʺ apart in double (1ʹ apart) rows.
Shallots (bulbs). Plant 6ʺ apart in rows 1ʹ apart.
Spinach. 1ʺ deep in rows 12ʺ apart. Thin plants to 6 – 8ʺ apart.
Turnips. ¾ʺ deep in rows 15ʺ apart.

Chapter Three

The Right Tool for the Job

Nothing is worse than trying to work with worn out, inadequate tools. Various kinds have evolved through the years and most will last a lifetime if given good care. Well-made tools are far from cheap, but a good investment in the long run. If you buy them as the need arises, a fine collection can be built up over the years. Auction sales of house contents can often prove useful, as the contents of garden sheds are sometimes 'sold for a song'. Keep an eye on the local papers!

A few basic tools

Spade
We always call it that! For trenching and general digging in winter and autumn. Choose one the right size for you, and if possible with a tread plate across the top of the blade. This prevents a lot of sole-destroying wear on the boots. Stainless steel spades cost a fortune but cut easily through the soil and need little or no maintenance.

Fork
Two kinds are needed: a narrow 'border fork' for work between plants — and the wife to dig with — and a wider one for general cultivation. Round or flat tined kinds are available, but the round sort are useful (very occasionally) when spiking the lawn.

Hoes
A swan-necked 'draw hoe' is the best tool for taking seed drills and some cultivation, and the flat-bladed Dutch hoe is great for weeding among other plants. Always walk backwards with this to avoid resetting the weeds. An old gardener we knew always called it the 'long handled watering can' because it stops also the soil cracking and losing valuable moisture. The three-pronged 'Canterbury Hoe' (which comes of course from Kent!) is great for general cultivation and taking out deepish drills or furrows.

Rakes
A well-made garden rake is the final tool for working the soil to a good tilth. Choose a sturdy specimen with a good forged head and avoid those resembling a row of nails! Also useful on the lawn is the spring-tined wire rake which can remove leaves and those dead grasses or 'thatch' and expend much energy.

Smaller hand tools

Trowel and fork

For planting and weeding in beds and borders. Choose a well made design which resists bending!

Secateurs

For pruning and general trimming. Various types available, including parrot-beak and anvil kinds. Price depends on quality, and cheap ones do not last long. Keep the edges sharp, oil the joints and never leave them lying around or even the best will soon be ruined!

Garden shears

Useful for hedges and general work, but electric trimmers make the job a lot easier and save hours of shear drudgery.

Bulb planter

Considered an essential tool by some gardeners but a trowel is preferred by us. Removes a plug of turf or soil which can be replaced when the bulb is planted, but stones can make life most difficult.

Odds and ends

Garden line

Vital for keeping the rows straight. Stick in a fork halfway across a long row. Choose a stout line with a wind-up holder and never leave out in the garden to rot!

Wheelbarrow

The gardener's friend! Avoid too heavy a barrow, and choose one with a wide wheel to stop it sinking in soft ground.

Trug

From nearby Sussex but useful in Kent for all manner of small carrying and collecting tasks. Quite expensive, but a coat of varnish when new will make it last for years and years.

Labels

Keep a range in various sizes. If pencil is used they are easily cleaned again for use next time. Many so-called garden pens soon fade.

Canes

A range of these from 3 to 8 feet long will suit most plants that need support. Very much cheaper if bought in bulk. Disinfect and clean the soiled ends before storage, to prevent wasteful rot and spread of disease.

Tying materials

Many kinds available, from plastic-covered wire to well-proven fillis twine. Use proper ties for trees so that damage is not done. Old tights can do a turn but tend to look a little out of place.

Mechanical devices

Lawn mowers

A choice far wider than any lawn! (See Chapter Eleven) Modern electric 'hover' types are fine for smaller lawns, but watch the safety aspect and use blades which cannot cut the feet. *As with all portable electric appliances outdoors, use an earth leakage circuit breaker to lessen risk of electrocution, and be sure it is placed at the house end of any extension lead.* Cylinder mowers are still the best for more areas and can achieve a high standard of lawnsmanship. Keep the cutters as high as possible at start and finish of season, and never so low as to scalp the growing areas. Regular maintenance is essential for long, trouble-free running.

Nylon line trimmers

Electric or petrol powered. Comparative newcomers to the garden scene which make short work of trimming the grass around walls, paths and trees, but always use protective goggles and take care to avoid damage to tender stems and idle bystanders.

Electric lawn rakers

These save much hard labour on the lawn when clearing leaves or removing 'thatch', but careful adjustment is needed or damage can soon be done! (See 'Laying a New Lawn')

Hedge trimmers

Perhaps the greatest labour savers of them all, but need great care in use. Sizes range up to 30 inches and can be single or double sided. Cordless kinds with rechargeable batteries are useful in remote locations, but charging times are long and battery life is all too short. Remove mains types from power before cleaning, and oil the blades before putting away.

Rotary cultivators

Found useful by many gardeners, but no substitute for proper digging. Never use where perennial weeds abound, or these will soon be spread by the growth from each tiny piece of root left in the ground. Beware of extended use of these machines, as a hard 'pan' can be produced below soil level, thus impairing drainage and proper growth of plants.

Storage of tools

Garden tools are a capital asset but soon depreciate if decay sets in. Dry storage is vital, but only works if the tools are cleaned and oiled after use. Wooden handles benefit from the occasional wipe with linseed oil which preserves the wood and improves their handling in use. Proper tool racks are ideal though expensive, and six-inch nails in lengths of timber can serve the purpose very well. Electric tools are even more affected by damp conditions, and should be stored well off the ground in a ventilated place.

Chapter Four

Manures and Fertilisers

Whatever is taken from the soil must always be replaced. Water is mostly restored by rainfall, but as plant nutrients are used they must be replenished, or growth and crops will suffer. The three main plant foods are nitrogen, phosphorus and potash (NPK), together with calcium, magnesium and sulphur. These are converted by the plant from natural or artificial manures or fertilisers into forms the plants can use. Additional elements are also needed in very small amounts, and these 'trace elements' (such as iron, manganese, molybdenum, boron, copper and zinc) are vital for healthy growth, though harmful if present in excess.

Functions of the three main foods
Nitrogen promotes green growth of stems and leaves, phosphorus encourages healthy rooting, and potash ensures good flowering and fruit.

Organic — or what?
A growing number of gardeners are turning today to plant foods free from possibly harmful chemicals, but bulky natural manures are comparatively low in certain nutrients and considerable quantities are needed for balanced growth. Some compromise is often the answer of course, with natural sources such as farmyard or horse manure being supplemented with occasional dressings of more concentrated kinds, which can either be quarried or factory made.

Bulky manures
Farmyard or stable manures are a rich source of humus but need high rates of application done in good time and are not always appreciated by less-keen neighbours. Avoid their use on ground where root crops are to grow, or 'sproggy' specimens are sure to result.

Poultry and other bird manures
Much richer, and best composted well before use or plants can be scorched. Use with care!

'It's elephants'.''

Garden compost
Excellent source of humus if well-prepared, but can contain weed seeds if insufficient heat existed in the heap (see section below).

Leaf mould
This was once the staple of many gardens and still a useful source of humus if the leaves are rotted really well.

Seaweed is a valuable source of plant nutrients and much used in many coastal areas.

'Artificial manures'
These range from simple chemical compounds such as sulphate of ammonia, to more complex formulations like the well-tried National Growmore introduced in wartime Dig for Victory days, well-remembered by older hands and still much used today. This has 7:7:7 nitrogen, potash and phosphorus, but many other kinds of fertilisers with different ratios of NP and K are available for various uses: e.g. higher nitrogen for grass and other green crops, and higher potash for tomatoes and flowering plants.

Liquid feeds
A solution of plant foods in water is a convenient way of feeding many plants. These can be in either powder or concentrated liquid forms and should always be used in accordance with makers' instructions, and only when the compost is moist. Such liquid fertilisers can also be used for foliar feeding of many plants through their leaves. A good drenching spray should be given, but never in bright sunlight because scorching may result.

Never exceed the stated dose!
It's tempting to give 'a little extra' when feeding plants, but this is wasteful and achieves no useful purpose. In fact, too great a concentration of salts in the soil can cause 'reverse osmosis' and removal of liquids from the plant tissues, leading to collapse and death of the plant. 'One for the pot' does not apply here!

Making your own garden compost
Far too much valuable garden 'waste' is destroyed each year by anti-social burning or consigning to the local tip. The greater part of these spent plants, clippings and suchlike can form splendid garden compost and add to the soil's fertility as well as saving money.

For the smaller garden, ready-made compost bins can be bought (at a price), but simple structures can often be fashioned from wood and other materials close at hand. Ideally, three such containers should be constructed alongside each other: one for collecting the current year's 'rubbish', the second containing the previous year's and rotting down, and the third's contents being used for feeding, mulching and general soil conditioning. All such containers should stand on the soil itself to encourage entry of the worm workforce. Bacteria play a major part though, and some air must be able to enter, but not so much as to stop high temperatures being reached. Start off the heap with a 9-inch layer of garden waste, and sprinkle over a dusting of proprietary compost accelerator or garden soil. This provides the nucleus of bacteria to do the breaking-down. Then continue with further layers in the same way, until the container is full and covered to keep in the heat and shield from too much rain. If grass cuttings (free from weedkiller) are used, make sure they are mixed with coarser material or a useless, slimy mass will result.

Chapter Five

Greenhouses are Great!

To extend the growing season and give somewhere to work in whatever the weather, a greenhouse has a place in almost any garden where it can be a source of profit and great pleasure — and a splendid hiding place! If a small amount of heat can be used, just to keep it frost-free, summer bedding plants can be raised from seed for a fraction of what they would cost if bought ready-grown later. And reliable crops of tomatoes, melons, cucumbers and many more can be harvested despite our changing Kentish weather.

Which one to buy?
Never rush out and buy the first greenhouse you see. It is a fairly major purchase, so plan things properly and be sure of just what you want. Look around the displays at garden centres and large stores throughout the county, where useful offers can sometimes be found. The smallest really practical greenhouse is about 8 feet by 6 feet but choose the largest size affordable that can fit in the space you have allotted. They can soon become quite crowded once the bug has bitten!

Metal or wood?
Aluminium-framed greenhouses are simple to erect, need a minimum of maintenance and are easily cleaned. Those with wooden frames are more expensive and need regular care, but can often be as much as 5 Fahrenheit degrees warmer than metal-framed ones of the same size. Fixing of polythene 'double-glazing' is also more easily done for saving heat in the winter months.

Where to put it?
Regular visits are needed at most times of the year, so site the greenhouse fairly near the house if you can. This also avoids long runs of electric cables and possibly water pipes, but never put it so near that it dominates the garden scene when viewed from the house. Choose a spot with as much sun as possible, and with some shelter from bitter winter winds. Avoid overhanging trees; leaves and falling branches can be rather a problem at times!

Avoid overheating

Fix the footings firmly!

The Great Storm of 1987 moved — and wrecked — many a greenhouse that had not been firmly fixed to the ground. A sturdy supporting base is vital, and also stops any settlement into the soil as time passes. Even quite a small greenhouse contains a great weight of glass, and will become distorted if some of it sinks in the ground. A 9-inch trench filled with concrete makes a good base, but be sure that it is square in all directions and perfectly level. Be sure to start with a layer of well-rammed stones in the trench to make a first-class job. For less permanent situations, steel or aluminium bases can be bought as an optional extra, and fixed to the ground with good metal stakes, well secured. We used old railway sleepers for one greenhouse and they have not moved an inch.

Plastic also has it points!

While glass has many advantages like long life and better retention of solar heat, a handyman can build a first-rate structure of corrugated plastic sheet fixed to a stout timber framework. Stiff and flat acrylic or polycarbonate sheets can also be used, as well as thick polythene sheet on a wood or tubular metal frame. Initial costs will be less than 'traditional' greenhouses but their life will be limited as the plastic ages in time, looks very tatty, and will have to be replaced.

Don't be caught bending!

To make full use of the space in any greenhouse, some form of staging is a must! This can be bought ready-made, but can easily be built with aluminium angle and slatted wood for a fraction of the cost. Do make sure the tops are well-supported; pots and boxes of plants weigh quite a lot — especially when well-watered. Portable staging makes for easy changes for different crops, such as in the summer when tomatoes are grown along one side.

Stand easy!

Provide a path of paving slabs inside the greenhouse. These not only improve the appearance and help to keep the floor clean, but during the day they absorb the sun's heat and give it out at night. The path can be quite wide, as although the soil borders help maintain moist air, their use for growing plants is not advised; diseases can build up in time unless the soil is changed.

Avoid overheating!

A greenhouse can be a snug haven in the colder months, but spring and summer sunshine sends the temperature sky-high to the distress or demise of many plants. Make sure that any greenhouse you buy has at least two vents in the roof and preferably a couple each side lower down to let in fresh air. Extra louvre-type vents can be bought for this purpose and are well worthwhile. Some degree of automation can be gained if automatic openers are fixed to the vents to increase ventilation as the temperature rises.

Too much of a good thing!
On very bright days the sun's rays can easily cause scorching and damage to greenhouse crops, and some form of shading is needed; either as roll-up slatted blinds outside, or a shading paint over the glass. These are easily applied with brush or roller, but choose a kind such as 'Coolglass' which is easier to clean off in autumn. If the greenhouse runs east – west, only the south side needs shading.

How about heating?
Although much can be done with an unheated or 'cold' greenhouse, if the winter's frost can be kept at bay, then the scope is widened greatly. Paraffin heaters were popular at one time and are still used by many gardeners, but modern, thermostatically-controlled electric fan heaters make life much easier. Natural gas is also used in some greenhouses, but like paraffin can produce much water vapour as it burns, needing extra ventilation which means loss of costly heat.

A minimum temperature of 40°F (5°C) is enough for most plants, and if the winter greenhouse is insulated inside with bubble-type polythene, losses will be kept to a minimum. But remember that an increase of 5 degrees is reckoned to double the cost!

Keep it clean!
The very conditions that make plants thrive in a greenhouse can also encourage pests and diseases to spread. Greenhouse hygiene is vital for healthy crops, and all dead or yellowing leaves and faded flowers should be removed and taken away before they cause troubles to start. Twice a year the whole house should be cleared of plants, washed inside and out with disinfectant, and fumigated to kill off pests in nooks and crannies. Removal of green algae from the glass also lets in more light as well as making the greenhouse a much better place to work in! This washing the greenhouse is nobody's favourite job and one for the oldest of clothes, but the sparkling sight of the structure when the job is done makes it all worthwhile. Really.

Chapter Six

Greenhouse Accessories

Propagators

To make the whole greenhouse warm enough to germinate seeds would cost a small fortune and is quite unnecessary. A simple heated propagator will provide the right conditions at a fraction of the cost, and is also ideal for striking many cuttings. Basically it is just a box with clear sides to let in light, a heating element (preferably thermostatically controlled), and some means of providing ventilation. No propagator is ever large enough at the height of the bedding-plant season, but the use of quarter-size trays for some of the seeds will save a lot of space. Cover the inside base of the propagator with fine gravel or sharp sand and keep it moist at all times. This gives more even heat distribution and helps maintain humidity. When using any propagator, examine the contents daily as growth is often rapid and plants may be spoiled if left inside too long.

The cold frame

Having a greenhouse is only half the story. Plants raised inside it may suffer a setback if planted straight in the ground outside, and should therefore always be 'hardened-off' first by placing in a cold frame outside. This can be quite a simple structure with a frame of aluminium or wood and sheets of glass. The top must be hinged or able to slide so that ventilation can be given, and gradually accustom the plants to the great outdoors. If appearance is not important, a serviceable but rather tatty-looking cold frame can even be made from stacks of turves, with an old window placed over the top! A cold frame can also be used for growing a wide choice of crops, including lettuce, melons and cucumbers. To prevent damage in high winds, a length of cord should be tied across the top so the sliding 'lights' stay firmly in place when closed at night.

Thermometers

Every greenhouse should have at least one maximum and minimum thermometer. This will allow a watch to be kept on those all-important night time temperatures without staying out there all night, and also ensure no undue heat is used, thereby wasting money. Hang the thermometer where it is shielded from direct sunlight and thus avoid misleading readings. It should also be firmly fixed to

prevent it being dislodged and broken when moving pots and plants around. A second max and min thermometer is useful, not only as a spare, but for checking the temperatures outside.

Ventilation

This is vital at most times of year and especially in spring and summer. A sudden burst of sunshine can send the temperature soaring into the nineties and beyond, and causing stress or damage to plants. Extra ventilators are a good investment, especially some louvre-type ones in the walls near the base. This will greatly improve air circulation as cool air can enter easily, to replace hot air passing out above. In recent years various kinds of automatic vent openers have been produced, and if properly installed they can do a useful job when the house has to be left unattended in the daytime. Some growers also favour an electric extractor fan which is usually fitted in a gable-end near the top.

Electricity

Although many gardeners still swear by paraffin for heating, electricity is far cleaner in use and more controllable. But any greenhouse wiring must be properly installed to professional standards to ensure absolute safety in the damp, earthy conditions which prevail. All sockets and switches must be waterproof, and all wiring of the correct type. Electric light is worth installing at the same time as jobs can then be tackled in the darker evenings too.

Heating

While an unheated or 'cold' greenhouse has many uses, its scope increases greatly if sufficient heat is given to keep the frost at bay. If such a 'cool' greenhouse has a minimum temperature of 40°F (5°C) most plants will survive, and if some form of polythene 'double glazing' is fitted up, heat (and money!) losses will be much kept to a minimum.

Thermostatic control is a great advantage as the cost of heating doubles with every extra 5°F. Electric fan heaters are highly popular these days as they distribute the heat well, and help maintain a buoyant atmosphere. These have their own integral thermostats, but a separate rod-type one can be used if properly installed. Frost warning devices are also available and these are worth considering if a number of valuable or irreplaceable plants is kept and the rest of the household is tolerant.

Water

This most essential commodity for any plants has usually to be carried from the house in cans. A water supply in the greenhouse might seem a luxury but has many advantages. Not only is much labour avoided, but the high pressure supply means that automatic watering and misting equipment can be installed, and holidays taken without worry! Such a supply must again be properly installed to comply with the water company's standards, and with pipes and fittings of the correct kind, buried to the required depth. If a standpipe and tap can be sited inside the greenhouse itself there will be less risk of frozen pipes in the winter.

Containers

Although some greenhouse gardeners still grow plants in the soil itself, this is not a good practice as diseases can build up with disastrous results in time. Nowadays some houses have a completely solid concrete floor, but borders of soil can still play a useful part in providing a moisture reserve to maintain humidity. On these borders can be stood large pots or boxes for the plants, or the peat-compost-filled growing bags are excellent for tomatoes and similar crops. The majority of greenhouse plants will be grown in pots, and although the old-fashioned clay kind had some advantages, plastic ones are preferred for most things. They are easily washed, lighter in weight and dry out less quickly in warm weather. Store them away from the greenhouse if possible, as they can provide ideal places for pests to hide in through the winter.

Composts

Confusingly, the word 'compost' has two distinct meanings in the gardening world. It can be the useful, humus-rich product formed in heaps from garden refuse (see chapter four), but it is also the quite different medium in which the plants are grown in pots and other containers. This compost falls mainly into two kinds: those based on some form of loam or soil, such as the John Innes mixtures, and the so-called soilless types based mainly on peat. Each kind has its advantages, but the peat-based ones are generally more popular. They are clean-working, light to handle and reliable, but dry out more rapidly than loam-based kinds which are heavier and more stable. Both kinds can be bought ready-made, or prepared to published formulae. Their ingredients do three main jobs; they hold sufficient water, allow good drainage and provide correct nutrients for the healthy growth of plants. Long-term storage is never recommended as the fertiliser contents can deteriorate, but bags of compost should be stored in a frost-free place to be ready for use when required.

Chapter Seven

Popular Greenhouse Vegetable Crops

Even an unheated greenhouse greatly extends the scope of gardening and enables flowers, foliage plants and vegetables to be produced far earlier than ever would be possible in open ground outside. The choice of what to grow in a greenhouse is a wide one, and depends on personal preference of the gardener concerned. But for most of us the first choice is generally the same; tomatoes of course.

Tomatoes

Always choose varieties developed for growing under glass. These include the well-tried Moneymaker, Ailsa Craig, Alicante and Shirley for medium-sized fruits, but for the best flavour the smaller-fruited Gardener's Delight is very well worth growing. Giant beefsteak tomatoes such as Big Boy or Dombito impress the neighbours and are full of flavour, but to achieve the maximum size, only a few trusses should be allowed to form on each plant. Tomatoes can be raised from seed if a minimum temperature of 55°F can be maintained to ensure they grow on without a check. Otherwise, plants of most common varieties can be bought later, all ready for setting out.

Growing tomatoes from seed

Fill a 3 inch pot to within half an inch of the rim with a good compost, space about six seeds evenly over the surface and sift some more compost over it to give about a quarter-inch covering. Put in a named and dated label, and stand the pot in a tray of water until the surface starts to glisten. Then cover with a piece of glass or polythene and place the pot in a heated propagator or on a warm windowsill. Remove the cover when the seedlings appear, and transplant into separate pots of a good compost when the first leaves unfold. Handle by the leaves to avoid damaging the sensitive stems, and set them so the leaves are only just proud of the compost. Keep in a light place to avoid leggy, drawn plants, and set out in their growing position when the first yellow flowers appear.

Growing on

In a new greenhouse, the border soil can be used if cultivated and manured well beforehand, but disease problems can occur if this is continued in following years and changing the soil is usually beyond

'Hello Big Boy.'

comprehension. Enriched-peat growing bags are popular with many gardeners nowadays, although their water-holding capacity is limited. Never put more than three plants to a bag or overcrowding will occur when they grow and spread their leaves.

Many keen gardeners are now turning to 'ring culture': an older method which still produces excellent results. This involves taking out a trench in the greenhouse border about fifteen inches wide, lining with strong polythene and filling with peat or an aggregate such as fine grit, gravel or coarse vermiculite. The plants are grown in bottomless pots or 'rings' which are stood at 18-inch centres on the material in the trench, and filled with a good potting compost. These rings can be purchased or made from roofing felt stapled together and with thin wire round the outside to keep them in place. Make the rings about nine inches tall and the same in diameter, and when filling, leave an inch headspace above the compost. The trench material is kept permanently damp by regular watering and only a liquid feed added to the compost in the rings.

Whatever growing method is used, delay feeding until the first tiny tomatoes have 'set'. This should happen about a week after the flowers have opened and can be encouraged by tapping the stems to help distribute the pollen. In the early stages an aerosol tomato setting spray can be used but this is not essential. Fertilisers used for feeding should be high in potash to encourage good fruit formation and faster ripening.

Growing support
For all but the spreading, bush-type tomatoes, some anchorage is needed as the plants grow. This is best done by inserting bamboo canes alongside each plant, and fixing to a wire running the length of the greenhouse. If growing bags are used, take care not to push the cane through into the soil beneath, or the roots will escape through the hole, possibly pick up disease and defeat their whole object.

As the plants grow taller, tie them loosely to the cane above each leaf joint, using soft jute twine or the plastic and wire twists which are snipped from a reel as required.

Regular removal of side shoots is also a must! These appear between each leaf stalk and the main stem and should be pinched out before they grow large and waste the plant's energy. Some will be missed; they always are, but can be cut out with a knife when spotted lurking down below.

Tomato troubles
Very few problems usually occur, and most of those that do are easily remedied if tackled in good time:

Blossom end rot. This develops as a leathery, dark brown patch at the end of the fruit opposite the stalk. It is caused by a combination of calcium deficiency and irregular watering early in the fruit's life, and can occur if the roots are allowed to dry out for even a short period.

Greenback. Otherwise sound tomatoes ripen unevenly, and part remains hard and green. Caused by too much sunlight and a shortage of potash, and avoided by shading the greenhouse and using a properly formulated food.

Mottled leaves. Yellowish patches on the leaves between the veins are a sure sign of magnesium deficiency and can be cured by drenching the plants to 'run-off' with a solution of two ounces of Epsom salts (magnesium sulphate) to a gallon of water.

Curling leaves. This often worries new growers of tomatoes but is quite normal especially in hot, sunny spells. As long as the leaves are in good colour they will soon uncurl when the stress is removed.

Pests and diseases

Pests are rarely a serious problem with healthy, well-fed tomato plants but when an infestation appears it should be dealt with quickly before it spreads.

Greenhouse Whitefly. Tiny, almost butterfly-like insects which rise in clouds if the plants are touched. Treat with a suitable insecticide for food crops, and repeat at three day intervals for two weeks to be sure of catching succeeding generations of this fast-breeding pest.

Tomato Moth Caterpillars. Not a common pest but has caused damage in Kent in recent years. The fruits are attacked by these voracious pests which can be killed with a spray of fenitrothion, but only use it several weeks before the fruits are picked; as with all sprays follow the manufacturers' instructions to the letter.

Botrytis or Grey Mould. A fungus disease in which a furry, grey growth covers the affected parts. These should be removed and burnt, and the plants sprayed with a fungicide. Botrytis usually occurs on damaged parts of the plants in the later stages of growth.

Cucumbers

The modern all-female kinds of cucumbers have made greenhouse growing of this useful crop far easier than once it was. In the past, all the male flowers had to be removed to stop formation of bitter cucumbers but mercifully we are spared this today.

Sowing

Sow the seeds singly in three-inch pots, setting the seeds on edge to reduce the risk of rot. Transplant to eight-inch pots of good compost when the plants have several true leaves, stand them on the greenhouse staging and grow up a framework of canes. Feed twice-weekly with a high potash liquid feed when the first fruits start to develop, and cut them as soon as they are large enough to use. This will encourage further fruit to form and ensure tender, tasty cucumbers for those delicious summer sandwiches.

Troubles are usually rare, but red spider mite may be a problem if the air becomes too dry. It helps to have a layer of gravel on the staging so that this can be kept moist and maintain humidity around the plants.

Sweet peppers or capsicums

An exotic but easily grown addition to the greenhouse crops. Raise from seed as for tomatoes, but grow on in five- or six-inch pots on the greenhouse staging. Feed twice weekly with high potash fertilizer and spray if greenfly are seen. Various varieties are available, from those with large almost oblong fruits, to perky small peppers ideal for patio containers or even window boxes.

Aubergines or egg plants

Raised from seeds as above, this subtly-flavoured vegetable is gaining popularity and does well in growing bags. Feed with high-potash tomato food when the tiny fruits begin to swell. Maintain humidity by spraying with water in dry spells to deter red spider mites, and cut as soon as the fruits have that rich purple sheen.

Salad crops

The greenhouse can really come into its own by providing the makings of salads to enjoy for healthy eating through the dark days of winter when prices are at their highest in the shops. Radishes and salad onions can be sown in any spare piece of greenhouse border soil, and even a sowing of quick maturing carrots will give useful roots for pulling when most tender and succulent. Lettuces are always welcome, and a crop can be ready for cutting at almost any time of year if the right varieties are chosen. Look out for Dutch varieties such as the splendid 'Kwiek' which was specially bred for growing through the winter in unheated greenhouses. The seeds are best sown first in Jiffy Sevens which are cunning compressed-peat discs within a nylon net. When soaked in water they swell to several times their dry height, and the seed is sown in an opening in the netting on top. As the young lettuce plants grow they can be planted complete in their Jiffy Sevens to grow on with no disturbance of roots.

Strawberries

A few pots of strawberry plants in the greenhouse can provide the first taste of these favourite fruits if a little work is done the previous summer. Look for some rooted runners from sound, healthy plants and put them in five-inch pots of John Innes No.2 compost. Water well, and leave in the cold frame until the turn of the year. Then move them into the greenhouse, water and feed, and pollinate with a soft brush when flowers appear. Keep feeding with a high-potash liquid feed, taking care to avoid soaking the plants' central crowns which might cause rot to develop.

Watercress

You do not need a crystal-clear stream of running water to grow this tasty crop so rich in minerals and vitamins! For some years now we've raised a steady supply for regular cutting in the greenhouse (and outside in a sheltered spot) by using a peat-filled growing bag.

Start by taking some pieces from a bunch of greengrocer's watercress and popping them in a glass of water on the window sill. The cuttings will root rapidly and can then be transplanted into the bag. As long as the peat is kept nicely moist the cress will grow quickly and is soon ready for cutting with scissors, all ready to serve after a rinse under the tap. An occasional liquid feed will help keep the crop flourishing, and the whole area is covered in next to no time. In fact you will be hard put to keep up with the plentiful supply!

Chapter Eight

Flowering Plants for a Kentish Greenhouse

One of the delights of greenhouse gardening is being able to produce a wealth of flowering plants to enjoy indoors in the colder months and outdoors in summer. The range of possibilities is vast, and the choice of course will depend on personal preference.

Greenhouse geraniums (pelargoniums)
Not to be confused with the hardy true geraniums or cranesbills, these more tender plants are of three main kinds: trailing or ivy-leaved, zonal and regal. Although susceptible to frost they can survive a winter minimum temperature of 40°F.

Propagation
Mainly from cuttings 3 – 4 inches long in summer. Cut below a leaf joint, remove lower leaves and place the cuttings around the edge of a labelled half-pot of 50/50 peat and sharp sand. Keep shaded until new growth indicates rooting has taken place. Move into 3-inch pots of good compost and grow on, taking care to keep them just moist. If kept too wet the stems will rot. Pinch out the growing tip when the plants are six inches tall, to encourage a good bushy habit.

Greenhouse geraniums can also be grown from seed, although these can be costly. Sow singly in separate small pots in a heated greenhouse propagator in January to be sure of summer flowering, and pot on when necessary.

Pests and diseases
Rarely much trouble, but leafhoppers and whitefly may attack the plants and need an insecticidal spray. Vine weevil grubs can attack the roots, and if these are a problem, treat with HCH. The disease black leg can affect plants grown in too damp conditions, and botrytis or grey mould may affect some plants. Remove affected parts and spray with a fungicide such as Benlate. Diseases are encouraged by crowding, and sufficient space should be left between plants to ensure a good circulation of air.

Feeding
Use a weak liquid feed at every watering, delaying this each time until the surface of the compost has dried out.

'What do you mean where have I been? I've been out to the green-house!'

Winter storage

Plants grown in pots should be kept as dry as possible with only occasional waterings to keep them 'ticking over'. Geraniums brought in for the winter from bedding displays outside must be lifted before the first frosts of autumn. They can be kept successfully in the minimum of space by cutting off excess, straggly growth and placing close together on a layer of soil in a wooden or plastic tray. If further fine soil is worked around the roots, and just kept barely moist through the winter in good light in the frost-free greenhouse, they will survive successfully until planting time in mid-May.

Repotting

This should be done in spring, but knock the plant from the pot first to be sure that roots are running round inside and really requiring a larger size pot.

Greenhouse primulas

Three main kinds are suitable for greenhouse cultivation if a minimum of 45°F can be maintained, and all can be treated in much the same way.

Primula kewensis

Grows to 15 inches and its attractive, scented yellow flowers are borne on upright stems from December to April. The leaves have a waxy, powdery appearance.

Primula malacoides (The Fairy Primula)

Attractive star-like flowers in a range of colours depending on the variety grown, and carried in whorls on slender stems.

Primula obconica

Lilac, blue, pink or red flowers ranging in size from 1 to 2 inches in diameter according to variety. Most attractive BUT the hairy leaves of this plant can cause a painful allergy resulting in a rash which spreads over hands and up the arms. It should NOT be grown by anyone with sensitive skin, and will even affect people not normally troubled by such things. Best avoided.

Propagation

Although perennials, these greenhouse primulas are grown from seed which is started in February or March. Sow very thinly on the surface of a peat-based compost in a 3-inch pot, and barely cover with sifted compost. Cover with glass or polythene, and germinate in a heated propagator at about 60°F. Transfer first to separate 3-inch pots and later to 5-inch for final flowering. When repotting take great care to keep the crowns of the plants proud of the surface, or they will tend to rot.

Gloxinias

With their striking, velvety, trumpet-shaped flowers and large dark green leaves, these most attractive and popular plants are easy to grow in the frost-free greenhouse, and will flower throughout the summer.

Propagation

Initially grown from seed sown early in the year, but germinate best around 70°F. Different named varieties are available and colours vary accordingly. Existing plants can be propagated by dividing the fleshy tubers in March, and potting up pieces with a stem attached. Stem and leaf cuttings can also be taken from established plants.

Begonias (tuberous rooted)

One of the most striking greenhouse plants, giving a dazzling show of blooms in brilliant 'poster' colours. They are also fine for patio pots in the summer time. These begonias are grown from tubers bought in early spring and placed hollow side upwards in moist peat in trays. Leave in a warm place until shoots appear, and then plant separately in 5-inch pots of a peat-based compost.

Chapter Nine

Keep it Safe!

Gardens seem safe enough places, yet every year hundreds of people of all ages are hurt, maimed for life or killed, in accidents which should never have happened. Constant care therefore needs to be taken to ensure good garden safety by checking the following points:

Sharp and pointed tools
Saws, knives and other sharp-edged tools should always be used carefully, stored away safely when not in use, and never left lying around. A useful maxim when using such implements is 'both hands behind the cutting edge whenever possible'!

Electrical tools
The great increase in garden power tools has made this the most hazardous area today. Always use a *residual current circuit breaker* which turns off the power if a fault like cutting a cable occurs. It should preferably be of the two-pole type, as these offer better protection in the case of a household wiring fault. Make sure the device is fitted at the power socket in house or garage, and *NEVER at the end of extension leads!* Check all connections at regular intervals and never make joints in damaged leads. Only use electrical appliances outdoors in dry weather, and take care to keep cables well away from cutting tools like mowers or hedge trimmers. Cordless, rechargeable trimmers and shears remove a lot of risk, but can still cause injury if switched on accidentally.

Chemicals
Always follow the makers' instructions, safely dispose of surplus spray and weedkiller solutions, and keep the containers away from young children and animals. Never store chemicals in other utensils; many are deadly if drunk, and for some there is *no known antidote*.

Garden ponds
A pond is a peaceful garden feature, but a magnet to youngsters who can all too quickly fall in and drown. Fencing or some form of stout netting cover is a help, but the only really safe pond where small children are concerned is one filled in with sand to become a play pit.

44

Greenhouses and frames

Site these away from main walkways where running youngsters might crash into them with fatal results. Cold frames made from double-skinned polycarbonate plastic sheet are costly but shatterproof and light to handle.

Barbecues and bonfires

Home cooking tastes even better out of doors, but be sure any portable barbecue is as stable as possible, and sited where it will not be overturned. Take extreme care when reviving dying embers, and always keep an extinguisher and fire blanket handy. Sudden flare-ups can be highly dangerous. Even a seemingly safe, burnt out bonfire can retain much heat — and seriously injure tiny feet which might stray through the ashes.

Motor mower exhausts and silencers are also dangerous hotspots, both to curious youngsters and when refilling empty petrol tanks. Allow to cool down before putting petrol anywhere near!

Canes and stakes

These can cause frightful eye damage when bending down to cut flowers or tend plants. They become a lot safer if small plastic bottles are placed on their ends.

Check round your garden today for possible hazards — and hopefully you and your visitors will enjoy a safe and happy gardening year!

'I see a great Fuchsia.'

Chapter Ten

Fuchsias are Favourite — says Bob

There are over 6,000 varieties of fuchsia, of which 110 are hardy and will grow in most gardens in Kent. All these have been hybridized from over a hundred of the species that grow mostly in South America, the West Indies and New Zealand. Most of them grow at between 8,000 and 10,000 feet on mountain sides in a temperature between 50° and 60°F and in a mist continually drifting over the mountain, so temperature control is important when growing cultivars.

It is also important to understand that fuchsias are a long-day plant, and must have ten hours of daylight in twenty four hours to grow and bloom well. It is possible to keep the plants blooming right through the winter under artificial light, but this can prove expensive. So the plant is allowed to go dormant in our autumn, and must be kept frost-free at all times.

Storing

This can be done in several ways: a heated greenhouse, which is expensive unless you have a lot of plants, a cool cellar which is ideal, or a cool bedroom which is quickly overgrown. At no time must the temperature get above 40°F or they will start growing. Check the pots once a month for water; more fuchsias are lost through under-watering than from any other cause. The best way to store them is to bury them under the bench in a cold greenhouse. In September, according to the weather, prepare to put them to sleep. Strip off the leaves and trim off a third of the wood. Water well, and make sure the label is clearly marked with the variety. They look very much alike without their flowers!

Dig out the soil under the bench so that when the plants are in the trench and covered with straw, at least four inches of soil will be needed to fill the trench. This can also be done in the open garden, but allow six inches of soil over the top. But wherever you do it, MARK THE TRENCH! I know of folks who are still looking for them! Standards can be laid in the trench; treat the top as you would a bush.

Starting off in the new year

On or about 1st February, get at least 45°F in the greenhouse, according to the weather. Remove all the plants from storage wherever they are, and bring them into good light. Spray the wood with lukewarm water and this will induce new growth — and the finer the spray the better. *DO NOT OVER WATER THE POT:* grow more on the dry side, and delay feeding until most of the shoots on the plant are in leaf. Any dead branches or tips can then be cut off.

I never keep any of the last year's plants after taking cuttings, as they tend to lose their vigour. And if you are showing you can get a better shape from a new cutting, and a better plant.

Cuttings

As soon as the new shoots are growing well, it is time to take cuttings. These need to be 1½ to 2 inches long, and cut off just under the leaf nodes. Strip off the bottom leaves, leaving the crown and two leaves on the cutting. It is now ready to plant. On no account hold the stem of the cutting, as the oil in your fingers can seal it. Hold it gently by the top leaves. Using a dibber or pencil, make a hole in the compost and insert the cutting. Push the dibber in again half an inch away from the cutting, and pull the soil towards it to exclude any air round the stem. With most fuchsias, rooting compound is unnecessary. You can use 1½-inch pots for one cutting or a 3-inch pot with cuttings all round the rim and one in the middle. With this method, use all the same varieties to avoid confusion when potting-on. Be sure to label well! Temperature: this needs to be between 50 and 60°F for the cuttings to strike well. Keep them out of direct sunlight until rooted; this will take about three weeks, and as soon as you see new green leaves in the centre, you will know the cuttings have rooted. If you only need a few plants, use this idea: get a plastic sweet jar from your sweet shop, and eight 1½-inch pots. Put one cutting to each pot as described above, label, water and insert all the pots in the sweet jar. Screw on the lid, label with the date and put the jar in good light but out of direct sunlight. Under the bench in a heated greenhouse will be fine.

Leave for two weeks, then unscrew the lid, and leave the jar for one more week, when the plants should be ready for potting-on. Use 3-inch pots. (There is no need to water the cuttings while in the jar.)

Potting on

Do not put a cutting into a pot larger than a 3-inch or you will lose it, but never allow young plants to get root-bound, as this will result in premature flowering. As soon as the roots reach the inside of the pot, move on to the next size up. I pot on 3 – 4 – 5 – 6-inch and stop at that unless making a standard.

Standards
These are best started from a cutting with three leaves instead of two. This is a triphylla cutting. Grow it in the normal way, but as soon as you pot-on to a 3-inch pot, put a small cane alongside it. As the plant grows, put a longer cane in the same hole and it will not damage the roots. Tie the plant to the cane every two inches. Leave the leaves on, but take out the shoots in the leaf nodes, up to the last three, depending on how tall you need the plant. I would suggest a half standard (30″) for a start. The last three shoots will form the head, and as they grow, pinch out the tip. And when the side shoots grow to four leaves, pinch the tip from these as well. After pinching the tip, the plant will grow another two inches.

Varieties
Four good hardy varieties for the garden, to be planted in June (and two inches deeper in the soil than in the pot, this is important), are Constance, Snowcap, Lena and Army Nurse.

Four basket varieties
It is as well to plant these early in March in order to be well grown for putting out after all danger of frost has gone. Ideally they need to be started in a greenhouse as good light is essential. (This also covers half baskets and hanging pots.) La Campanella, Eva Boerg, Laurie and Pink Marshmallow.

Four good varieties for growing as standards
(If you are going to try a standard I would advise you not to try a full standard, as this can take two years. Go for a half standard — which is 30 inches high.) Look for a triphylla cutting (three leaves instead of two. See the section on cuttings). Ting a Ling, Constance, Royal Velvet and Frank Saunders.

Feeding
After potting-on from the cutting stage into 3-inch pots, feeding must commence and a high nitrogen feed is essential. I use Chempak No.2 but if you use a feed with high potash content, only feed the plant half as much until the flower buds appear, or the wood will harden and the flowering period will be short.

As soon as the buds appear, I switch to a high potash feed such as Chempak No.4, plus a monthly feed of Chempak No.2 to keep the plant growth green.

Pests

Whitefly

To beat this pest you need a programme! Spray with a knock-down spray on Monday, Wednesday and Friday. This will not only kill all the whitefly but the eggs as well. Or you can use a systemic spray which will enter the leaf. Do not use it on food vegetables.

Greenfly

Use the same knock-down spray, but once will be enough.

Thrips

Severe attacks can ruin the growing tips, and as a precaution, spray with pyrethrum or malathion in the growing stage.

Red spider mite (not a spider!)

If the attack is small, use a fumigant smoke, or spray malathion. To prevent red spider working, keep the floor damp in warm weather.

Vine weevil

The first you will know of this is when the plant falls over, owing to the roots being eaten. To prevent this happening, mix HCH dust with your compost. Failing that, mix up a systemic insecticide in a watering can to the instructions on the bottle, and water the plants in the normal way.

Botrytis

This is a fungus disease and is probably the worst thing that can happen in your greenhouse. It consists of a grey mould, and you will get it when the house is cold and damp. Other contributory factors are overcrowding and lack of cleanliness of pots, trays, staging or floor. Use a fungicide smoke if the plants are very damp, or a fungicide spray if the house is fairly dry.

Rust

This is shown by rust coloured pustules under the leaf. Always check for this disease before buying a plant, or you will spread it in your greenhouse and there is no rust cure on the amateur market.

To sum up, all fuchsias should be removed from the greenhouse when the temperature gets high in the summer. Out in the garden will do, but not under trees as red spider can attack from these. Make yourself a shade house with green small-mesh netting: not only will it shade the plants, but it stops the wind damaging them.

And at all times DO NOT overwater!

Chapter Eleven

Lawns

No other single feature in a garden can make such a difference as the lawn. Whatever its size, a well-tended stretch of grass can improve even the dullest garden's appearance, as well as giving space for exercise or relaxation.

Starting a new lawn

Preparation pays dividends in all garden work but nowhere more than with lawns. The site should be level and flat, and preferably not shaded by trees for much of the day. It must be well cultivated by digging to remove all traces of perennial weeds, or these will be a constant source of trouble later on. Once this is done, the ground should be firmed with the heels, working slowly across the plot, and followed by raking to fill in hollows and remove bumps. These two steps should be repeated several times, and the final result is best checked on a sunny evening when the slanting rays will soon show any shortcomings before giving up for the day. At the final raking, work in about 2oz of a general fertilizer such as Growmore to each square yard.

Turf or seed?

Both can give first-class results, but turf gives a virtually instant lawn and can be laid at almost any time of year, providing the ground is not frozen or covered with snow. Even indifferent turf is more expensive than seed, and unless the very best kinds are used the final lawn will never be as good as that from a quality mixture of best grass seed.

Laying turf

Arrange for the turf to be delivered when laying can begin. It soon deteriorates if left for more than a couple of days. The ground should be moist when laying the turf, and as work proceeds stand or kneel on a stout board or plank to avoid making hollows with your knees. Pull the turves in tight with a rake, and place the next layer staggered to give a bonding effect like brickwork so the turf knits together. Gently firm down each row with the back of the rake to ensure complete contact with the ground below.

Cut the turves where necessary with a spade or edging iron, and sift some fine soil over the surface when laying is done. If this is

'I told you the grass was long!'

carefully brushed across the surface with a stiff broom it fills in the cracks and ensures an even surface. In dry spells be sure to keep the new turf moist by gentle spraying with a sprinkler, and test at intervals by gently lifting a turf to see if the grass is rooting into the soil beneath.

When to sow

There are two times of the year when grass seed can be sown successfully; in spring and the end of summer/early autumn. The latter time is best as the soil is warm from the summer sun, germination will be rapid as long as the soil is moist, and the grass will have time to become established before winter sets in.

Choice of lawn seed

One advantage of using seed is that suitable kinds of grass can be chosen for the use the lawn will get. For a hard-wearing general-purpose lawn or family football pitch, a mixture containing the new dwarf ryegrasses is worth considering. The very finest grasses are good for purely ornamental lawns, but need much maintenance. Special mixtures are obtainable for lawns in shady places where ordinary grasses struggle, give up and die.

Sowing the seed

Choose a still day when the raked soil is nicely moist but not wet, and scatter a matchboxful of seed evenly to each square yard. If the area to be sown is not too large, it helps to lay out a grid of strings a yard apart for this stage. Finally rake the soil to cover much of the seed, gently firm with the back of the rake and if possible arrange netting or other protection against hungry birds which can also ruin the surface by using it as a dust bath.

Keep the young grass growing by using a gentle sprinkler in dry spells and delay mowing until about an inch and a half tall, when it should just be tipped with a very sharp mower. This and the light rolling action of the mower will encourage the grass to 'tiller' or grow more shoots from the base.

General lawn care

Choosing a mower

A bewildering array of mowing machines greets the beginner in any garden centre, but the choice will always be partly decided by the area of grass to be mown. For small lawns, mains-powered mowers can be of hover, wheeled-rotary or cylinder design, and all include models with a rear roller to produce the striped effect sought by many gardeners. Whatever kind of electric mower is chosen, always use an earth leakage circuit breaker for extra protection in the event of cut mains cables. This device must be installed at the house end of the cable. For larger lawns, petrol driven mowers offer freedom of movement without cables, at the cost of greater noise, but modern mowers are designed to keep this to a minimum. For the finest finish, the traditional cylinder mower is acknowledged to be the best, but where grass is allowed to grow high and untidy between mowing, the wheeled-rotary mower comes into its own. Its spinning blade cuts through the longest stems and blows them into the collecting bag, whereas a cylinder mower tends to flatten tall stalks and leave them to spring up after passing on its way.

Using the mower

At the height of the growing season, lawns should be cut twice weekly to maintain a quality finish, but where this cannot be done, resist the temptation to cut too short in the hope of saving work. If the mower is set to a minimum cut height of one inch, the grass will flourish and be far better able to withstand long dry spells. Opinions differ regarding removal of cuttings from the lawn. If they are collected and mixed with coarser garden refuse they will form useful compost or may be used as a mulch. On the other hand leaving the cuttings where they lie will return nutrients to the grass, help reduce drying of soil, and save much cartage of cuttings. The big disadvantage to many is the quantity of cuttings carried indoors on the family's feet.

Feeding

Too many gardeners seem to forget that grass is a crop like any other and continually takes food from the ground. Whilst leaving the cuttings on the surface helps to some extent, nutrients are continually leached out by rain and need replacing if the grass is to flourish. When growth starts in spring the main requirement is nitrogen for good leaf growth, and a fertiliser for use at this time should have a far greater proportion of this than the other main foods phosphorus and potash. Some fertilisers contain part of their nitrogen in a form released slowly over a period, and although more expensive, such mixtures make feeding a far less frequent task. Lawn foods can be applied as granules by hand or a wheeled distributor, or in liquid form using a watering can with dribble bar or a hose end dilutor. Solid feeds can scorch the grass if left too long on the surface, and should be applied just before rain, or watered-in if dry conditions prevail. Autumn lawn feeds can help maintain the vigour through the winter when growth is slow. These contain a far lower proportion of nitrogen as lush grass is not required and could even encourage disease.

Lawn weeds

These can be the bane of a keen gardener's life, but selective lawn weedkillers can eliminate most with a few applications. Such chemicals work by affecting the growth of broad-leaved weeds and function far better when the weeds are growing well in May or early June. Strictly follow the makers' directions and guard against risk of drift to nearby plants. Greenhouse crops such as tomatoes can be affected by just a trace of these weedkillers, so avoid walking in with weedkiller on the wellies! Leave these weedkillers to dry before allowing children or pets on the lawn, and avoid using collected grass as a mulch for the next two mowings.

Moss

This is tolerated by many gardeners as it is green and invisible at a distance. Its presence usually betrays bad drainage and, although proprietary mosskillers work well, the underlying cause should always be removed if possible. Spiking the lawn in winter is a strenuous job but can help greatly to remove surface water and improve aeration of the soil beneath.

Scarifying

In time, a layer of dead grasses forms below the sward and this can spoil the lawn by stifling growth, withholding moisture and impairing drainage. Its removal is another arduous task with a spring-tined rake, but electric lawn rakers make the job a practical one on even large lawns. Avoid setting the whirling tines too low or more grass will be removed than thatch! The material collected makes a useful addition to the compost heap.

Lawn edges

However smart the lawn itself, it will never look its best with rough and ragged edges. Trimming these can often take longer than mowing the lawn, but is generally a far less frequent task. Long-handled shears can save much bending, and if adjacent to beds and borders the edge should slope slightly to lessen the risk of its being broken away when walked along. Where paving stones adjoin the lawn a half-moon edging iron can soon produce an immaculate edge with minimum effort if the blade is kept good and sharp.

'If we can just find the car we're O.K.'

Chapter Twelve

Garden Ponds

The sight and sound of water can add interest and enjoyment to any garden and, not surprisingly, ponds have become increasingly popular in recent years. They can range in size from tiny pools forming a decorative feature, to large ponds of almost lake-like size. A wider range of plants can be grown, fish can flourish and many ponds can play a useful part in conserving wildlife now that many natural Kentish ponds have disappeared. Almost their only drawback is the danger element, and any gardener should think twice before making a pond where small children are likely to be at large. In such cases existing ponds might be better converted to sandpits or bog gardens until the risk has gone with the passing of years.

Siting a garden pond

A pond's position is often dictated by the shape and size of its surroundings, but certain points should be considered before a decision is made. To look most natural a pond should preferably be in a garden's lowest part, and also sited away from trees to avoid trouble from falling leaves in autumn. But such ideals are not always possible, and although extra work may be involved, most places are better than none at all.

Choice of materials

At one time all garden ponds were of concrete construction and some are built in this way today. Their cement linings can sometimes stay leakproof for many years, but hard winters can take their toll and the damage is rarely easy to repair. Nowadays most gardeners choose to make their ponds in one of two ways: by using a preformed, moulded pool which is simply sunk in the ground, or with a strong, flexible liner sealing an excavated and shaped hole.

Preformed pools are of two main types: cheaper, vacuum-formed plastic or the more expensive kind fashioned from fibreglass. The plastic ones are light and easy to handle, but their flexibility often causes problems when filled with water unless great care is taken to ensure complete support. Preformed fibreglass pools suffer from no such defects and are invariably a better investment.

Installing a preformed pool

Painstaking work at this stage will be well repaid by many years of trouble-free service, and the extra time taken is very well spent. Begin by excavating a rectangular hole several inches bigger than the pool at its largest dimensions, and give temporary support with a few bricks while levels are adjusted. This levelling is vital: otherwise the pond will look extremely odd when filled with water later on. Sand or gravel is best for filling in around the pool as this can flow more easily than garden soil and is quickly poked into place to ensure complete support. It helps to have the top edge an inch or so below ground level before backfilling starts, as the pool invariably rises slightly during the process. Finally check levels again with a board and spirit level before filling the pool with a hosepipe.

Flexible liners

These have the great advantage that the pond can be of almost any desired shape and size, and with shallow shelving around the sides to support the marginal plants. The depth of the main pool is decided by whatever its future occupants are to be: whilst common or garden goldfish are happy with a depth of eighteen inches or so, some ornamental fish prefer double this. If too shallow the pond might freeze solid in hard winters and then few if any fish would survive. Having planned the pool, the size of liner must be calculated by measuring along cross sections at the widest points and allowing a foot or more overlap for securing all round the top. Check — and double check — the measurements to ensure that no mistakes are made. It is too late once you have cut the liner! Stout gauge polythene is sometimes used for lining ponds, but its life is limited to a few years before it becomes degraded and starts to leak. PVC liners last at least twice as long, but the best by far are those made from butyl rubber. These are far more expensive still, but well worth considering for a permanent pond.

Installing the flexible liner

Once the desired shape has been excavated and is perfectly level all round, great care must be taken to prevent possible damage to the liner by those inevitable stones in our Kentish ground. Ideally the whole should be lined with a smooth coating of a couple of inches of soft sand, followed by a covering of damp newspaper several sheets thick. Some folk favour old carpet, but this is sometimes difficult to fit snugly in the hole. The liner is then placed over the excavated site and held loosely by bricks laid round the outside. Filling with a hosepipe is then begun, and the lining is gradually pulled into position by weight of water as the level rises, care being taken to deal with creases as they form. Finally trim round with stout scissors to leave a surround of about a foot of liner.

Stocking the pond
Concrete ponds need treating with a special sealant before filling and stocking, but with preformed pools and liners the work can proceed at once. Pond plants are not cheap but good, healthy specimens are worth buying to prevent any problems later. Underwater oxygenating plants play a vital part in maintaining a suitable environment for fish and other creatures in the pond. These might include the tough Canadian pondweed (Elodea canadensis) and the related Elodea crispa (Lagarosiphon major) which is said by many to be the best of all. Such plants are kept submerged by winding lead wire or strip around them and should be allowed to root for a couple of weeks before fish, which might well otherwise destroy them, are introduced. Plants such as the water buttercup are also useful as their underwater parts play an oxygenating rôle. These should be planted in plastic baskets lined with hessian and filled with good garden loam. After firmly planting them, top with a layer of gravel to avoid disturbance and place gently in position on the shallower shelf surrounding the pool.

Water lilies flourish at different depths according to their type, and this information should be obtained when the plants are purchased. They are most attractive and also play an important part in providing shade for the pond's population.

In an established pond, something like 60 – 70% of the surface area should be covered. Water lilies need lifting, dividing and replanting after a few years and the time for this is often heralded by some of their leaves being thrust above the surface.

Fish for a garden pond
These creatures are a constant source of interest and with regular feeding in a well-maintained pond will often live for years and raise many broods of young. They should only be put in after the oxygenating plants have become well established. Whether they are cheap goldfish or the costly Koi carp, buy good disease-free fish from a reputable supplier and choose from among the many kinds described in specialist literature. When introducing any fish, leave the plastic bags in which they are swimming, immersed in the pond until their temperatures are the same.

Installing a pump in the pond
Many gardeners find the sound of moving water an added attraction
and putting a pump in the pond is a fairly simple job. These can
either just work a fountain, or with extra piping will enable a
waterfall to be added. Electricity and water can form a lethal
mixture, and any installation must be done to professional standards
by a competent electrician, making sure that a residual current
circuit breaker is incorporated.

Finishing touches
Any preformed pool or flexible liner needs covering round the edges
to conceal it and give an attractive appearance. Overhanging paving
slabs can fill the bill but proper anchorage is needed to stop them
tipping up! Such edging is easy on a straight-sided pool, but on
curved edges the slabs will need some shaping. This can be done
gently with a hammer and bolster or an angle-grinder should one be
available.

Maintaining the pond
Although pond snails and other creatures play a small but useful part
in maintaining a thriving pond, periodic attention is vital to prevent
overcrowding by plants and accumulations of invading blanket
weed. This is best removed by winding a rough stick round and
round and pulling it out. Autumn leaves can be a problem if allowed
to sink to the pond's bottom where they rot and pollute the water.
Protect the pond with netting or remove before they accumulate.

The pond gardener's year

Winter
As winter approaches and cold weather comes, the fish will be less
active, and their need for food and oxygen falls. They can survive the
cold and exist in a state of torpor, living off their fat. They will be at
risk if the pond freezes over. A skin of ice that melts during the day is
no problem, it is the ice that persists for weeks or days that is the
danger. It stops the oxygen getting in, and the gases in the water
cannot escape. If the pond contains any decaying material these may
include methane and hydrogen sulphide and this can kill the fish.
Never smash the ice with a hammer or other blunt instrument as this
will cause shock to the fish and could kill them. Many pond liners
each year are punctured with stakes or garden forks so take care
when poking about at this time.
 Before freezing begins in autumn, float a couple of children's play
balls on the surface. A hole will be left when ice forms, and this

should be kept open every day. If you have an electric supply to a pump, attach it to a small pond heater and place under a float.

Thick ice damages concrete ponds in much the same way as it bursts pipes, and a heater can prevent this. If no heater is available, one corner of the pond should be covered with clear polythene, supported underneath by floating logs or polystyrene boxes with water in them. If the pond is small cover it all in the same way.

Spring

As the ice disappears, the fish will begin to move. If you have a heater in the pond, leave it on to raise the temperature. The fish now need food as their reserves and resistance to disease are low. The higher temperature will encourage them to feed. Fungus is the disease most likely at this time of year, and little can be done about that until the fish are feeding. Be ready to feed them as soon as you see them foraging. Chopped earth worm and flake feed need to be fed as much as they will take. Feeding a varied diet will restore the fish and they will soon begin to breed. The pellets for feeding Koi carp are the best for all fish. At this time a half change of water is very beneficial and all ponds should have this done as soon as possible.

Summer

Late spring or early summer is the time for cleaning out the pond. Remove all accumulated rubbish, and when doing this be careful of small fry. It is best to put it into a wheelbarrow as these can then be spotted and saved. Put in new plants, clean up old ones and add fertilizer to the baskets. Be vigilant at this time of the year for signs of the Great Diving Beetle (Dytiscus marginalis) as its larvae will eat fry as well as adults. Do not remove all beetles, only the large ones, and if green fly and other pests are on the plants, lay something on them to submerge the leaves and the fish will eat them. Remove it the next day for the plant to get air.

Blanket weed can be a problem, even in ponds which have never had it before, as the spore is airborne, and is best removed with a stick from the hedge twirled round in the weed, but check for snails and fry before putting it on the compost heap.

A measure of control can be obtained by using Allclear tablets, Jungle Blocks or Algizin P, but the debris will fall to the bottom and de-oxygenate the water.

If your pond has many fish, consider building a reserve pond. This will help by holding the fish when cleaning out, and you do not have to be in a hurry to get them back again.

Autumn

This is the time to reduce most of the dead or dying plant growth to a minimum, and all oxygenators will have ceased to work. If left they will cause problems over winter, and this should be done by mid-September at the latest.

All fish should now be in good condition, and feeding continued to build up their winter reserves.

As they have been in that water for months, and many waste products have accumulated on the bottom, it is time to half change the water again. This is essential if the pond is well stocked with fish.

Having done that, if the bottom of the pond has no cover for the fish, some pieces of plastic or clay pipe laid in the bottom will give them all the cover they need. Herons and gulls will be working all year round.

Remove the pump if fitted, and connect a heater ready for hard weather.

Cover the pond with a fine mesh net to catch falling leaves, and remove these to let in light as soon as leaf fall has finished.

Chapter Thirteen

Making and Stocking a Sink Garden

Old sinks make splendid settings for many small plants, especially most alpines, and can be a constant source of interest. Original stone sinks are nowadays costly and hard to find, but the white porcelain kind can be made to look most effective by coating them with 'Hypertufa'. This is a mixture of two parts of sifted peat to one each of sharp sand and cement (all parts by volume), thoroughly mixed and watered to the consistency of a rich fruit cake mix.

Siting the sink
Aim for a mainly open sunny position away from overhanging trees, which can cause problems with leaf fall in autumn. These sinks are very heavy and are most easily moved on their side, using pieces of broomstick or pipe as rollers underneath like the ancient Egyptians!

Coating the sink
The surface should be thoroughly cleaned, but no roughening is required. The coating described above is held in place with a PVA building adhesive such as Unibond, applied with a brush and allowed to become tacky. It is most important only to treat about a foot of the sink's surface at a time, or the adhesive will dry out too soon. The mix is best applied with gloved hands, pressing gently into place and making the covering no more than half an inch thick at the most. If too thick it will slide down and fall off. Continue over the top and down inside for a few inches. Avoid too smooth a finish so the final result has a rustic 'stony' appearance. To prevent any damage to the coating, the work is best done in the sink's final position, with it standing on a brick at each corner. Pieces of hardboard are useful, laid around the job as work proceeds, so that any fallen mixture can be retrieved and used again. The coating hardens quite quickly, but should be left shaded from direct sun or driving rain for several days. This Hypertufa is amazingly long-lasting; some of our sinks have now withstood the worst of winters over the past twenty years.

Try to slope the sink slightly towards the plughole, and put in a layer of largish stones, followed by some gravel to ensure good drainage. For most plants, the main filling can be John Innes Potting Compost No. 1, plus a quarter of its volume of small stone chippings mixed well in. Or make up a similar mix with 7 parts of good loamy

'*Perhaps a few plants would do it.*'

topsoil, (preferably sterilised), 3 parts of peat, and 2 of sharp sand, adding 4oz of John Innes Base Fertiliser and ¾oz of ground chalk or limestone to each bushel of mixture. Then mix in the chippings. A few well-shaped stones set in the surface can add interest and also provide a measure of shelter for tender or crevice-loving plants.

Choice of plants
Any lime-tolerant plants should grow well in the mixtures described above. In all but the very smallest sink garden, a tiny dwarf conifer can be a useful feature, but choose a very slow-growing one! The small juniper communis 'Compressa' is ideal, and should be no more than a foot high after ten years. Most garden centres stock a wealth of other suitable plants: sempervivums (house leeks) and small mound-forming saxifrages look good, as do dwarf gentians, true geraniums, pinks, thrift and some of the sedums. Small bulbs such as miniature narcissi and irises are effective in spring, and miniature roses in summer if space permits. A selection of thymes can be planted around the edges to trail over the side, or use Gypsophila repens. Cover the remaining bare soil with a layer of flint grit to keep the surface dry around the plants. Alpines are hardy customers but they do detest damp!

Good labels are a great help in keeping track of small plants in such places as sinks, but the ordinary white kind can look unsightly. Far less conspicuous are the plastic labels from Mac Penny. They have a black surface on one side, which is scratched with the metal-tipped stylus provided, to give white letters which cannot fade or wash off.

Keeping the sink tidy
Untended sinks can soon look scruffy, but the careful attention needed to keep them looking good is one of the attractions of such plantings. Remove dead plants and surrounding soil, followed by fresh soil when replanting. Check under the chippings in dry spells and water thoroughly if needed. Give an occasional feed of a slow acting fertilizer such as hoof and horn or a weak liquid feed, but keep to a minimum to avoid excessive growth.

Chapter Fourteen

The Kentish Fruit Garden

'Kent, sir — everybody knows Kent — apples, cherries, hops, and women' — Mr Jingle in 'Pickwick Papers' — Charles Dickens

Most gardens, whatever their size, offer space for growing at least some fruit, and modern rootstocks pioneered by our own Institute of Horticultural Research at East Malling have made it possible to fit in far more than could ever have been done in Dickens' days. Gone are the days of large, 'standard' orchard-size trees which dominated the garden, were hard to prune or spray and so never gave a worthwhile yield. Modern, small trees on dwarfing rootstocks are completely manageable, attractive and highly productive.

Apples
The most space-saving form of these popular fruits are the CORDONS: long, single stems trained up slanting 8ft cane at 45 degrees, attached to supporting wires fixed to stout posts. The trees are planted 2 – 3 feet apart, making sure the union where the graft was made is about 5 inches above soil level. Where a wall or fence is available FAN or ESPALIER forms can be grown. In the open ground, dwarf pyramid fruit trees are easily maintained, but be sure the rootstock is a genuine dwarfing kind such as M.26. The latest kind are the COLUMNAR apple trees which produce their fruit on a single upright stem which needs no pruning. At present only a restricted number of special varieties are available in these columnar trees. There is a wide choice of varieties obtainable in normal forms. Cox is everyone's favourite apple, but not an easy one for the garden. The catalogues list many alternatives, and the new kinds from East Malling such as Fiesta, Kent, and Greensleeves are well worth growing.

Cherries
These were at one time the staple fruit crop of Kent but were difficult in most gardens because of the size of tree. In recent years, much smaller cherry trees on the dwarfing rootstock 'Colt' have made them a far better proposition for the garden. They are easily protected from marauding birds with netting, and can be picked

without risking life and limb on tall ladders. Colt is not completely dwarfing though, and trees may reach a height of eighteen feet unless grown as centre leader bushes with two tiers of branches at three and five feet. Flower buds will then be confined to the lower parts of the tree and netting should be possible for the first ten years at least.

Soil
Cherries favour a well-drained, medium, slightly acid loamy soil but will do quite well on any but those which are shallow or badly drained. They can be fan trained to conserve space, and when grown this way, should be planted 15 feet apart. Pruning is done in spring as the flowers begin to appear, and a dressing of 3oz of Growmore to each square yard should be applied around the trees in February. Spray with tar oil wash in winter to kill over wintering pests, or use dimethoate when the buds are white. Popular varieties include Merton Glory and Van which pollinate each other, Stella which pollinates all others, and the self-fertile cooking cherry Morello.

Currants
Of the three kinds of currants, blackcurrants are grown more commonly than red or white. All are self-fertile, take up a relatively small area and crop in the year after planting. No soil is too rich for blackcurrants, and they can be fed plenty of nitrogenous fertiliser. They prefer good drainage but also a soil that retains moisture. When fruit has formed they need copious amounts of water.

Red and white currants withstand drought better, and are less greedy of nitrogen, otherwise their needs are similar. Red and white currants flower early, so should not be planted in a known frost pocket.

Blackcurrants tolerate being planted under trees, but this delays ripening. A sheltered site is preferred as this encourages pollinating insects to work if flowering time coincides with bad weather. The bushes have a productive life of 10 – 12 years according to feeding.

Blackcurrants' season is from July to September according to variety, and the fruit is borne on the previous year's wood. So when pruning, and as soon as the crop has been cleared, take out all the wood that bore fruit that year. Red and white currants' season is from June to July and the fruit is formed on the old wood. So cut out the new at pruning time. Plant one to two year old bushes between October and March. Plenty of well rotted manure or mushroom compost with 3 – 4oz of Growmore added should be dug in before planting. Do not plant too deeply, only two inches of soil is needed over the roots. Water in well. Planting distance is three feet apart, and do not allow weeds to take water and nutrients from around them.

Two good blackcurrants to grow for early cropping are Tor Cross and Blackdown. For late blackcurrants go for Malling Jet or Amos Black. Among the redcurrants, Malling Redstart or Minnesota are good, and both are early cropping. White Versailles is a good white.

Against pests such as aphids, blackcurrant leaf midge and red spider mite spray with Malathion. For leaf spot and mildew use Nimrod T.

Gooseberries
Native to Britain where they have been cultivated since the thirteenth century. They are self-fertile and ideal for the small garden. Gooseberries are tolerant of most soils but not waterlogging, and are sensitive to potash deficiency. Planting time is from November to February, on ground well enriched with farm yard manure, mushroom compost or your own compost with general fertilizer added. Plant 3 – 4 feet apart according to variety, and cover the roots with 3 – 4 inches of soil. If dry, water in well. Keep the soil weed-free by shallow hoeing or you will damage the roots. Gooseberries demand high potash, particularly in light soils. Potash deficiency causes poor growth and early defoliation. Wood ash worked in lightly will help, but a dressing of sulphate of potash at 1 – 2oz to the square yard in spring is preferred.

Avoid promoting lush growth by the use of nitrogenous fertilizers, as this may cause mildew. Prune the bushes in early spring, taking out any crossing branches and leaving the centre open with room for a blackbird to fly through. Having done that, mulch the bushes with dung or compost. Gooseberries can be grown as bushes, standards or columns. With the column, all the fruit is on the outside and makes for easier picking. Gooseberry troubles include aphids, sawfly and mildew. Both the former can be dealt with by sprays, and mildew can be avoided by proper pruning or spraying with Benlate as soon as it is seen. Many good varieties can be had, but try Malling Invicta as a second early. Raised in 1967 it has proved popular and is mildew-resistant. Careless and Leveller have been about for years and are still grown, as is Lancashire Lad — a red-fruited variety.

Peaches and nectarines
Bush peaches and nectarines are hardy in the south of England, but need the protection of a south facing wall. Both fruits need plenty of sun but do better under glass or polythene. Those under glass rarely have peach leaf curl.

Planting
A well-drained, deep loamy soil gives the best results. Soils with a high lime content are disliked.

Apply bonemeal at the rate of ½lb per sq yd, and work in well. If the tree is container-grown do not plant deeper than it was in its container. Bare rooted trees should be planted to a level at least four inches below the graft union.

Planting time: Mid October to mid March. Keep the plant at least four inches away from the wall, and tie the tree to it temporarily. If staking, put the stake in the hole before planting.

If more than one tree is planted, leave 15 feet between the trees.

When planted, mulch as soon as possible with dung or compost. In the first year rub off the blossom.

Do not plant in a known frost pocket, as the tree flowers in February or March. Wall trees can be protected with HESSIAN at night, but remove it during the day to allow pollinators access to the flowers.

Fan-grown trees tend to give an excessive crop and must be thinned to one peach per sq ft, and nectarines one to every nine inches square . . . Copious watering is needed while the fruit is swelling, especially under glass.

An annual feed of 4oz per sq yd of balanced fertilizer should be given in summer.

Pruning. When pruning, remember that peaches and nectarines fruit on the previous year's wood, so prune them hard to induce plenty of new growth. However do not go to the other extreme, as excessive pruning induces lush growth.

Cut out any dead or crossing wood, tying back if a wall trained plant. Over-vigorous trees should be root pruned.

Peaches and nectarines are prone to peach leaf curl, brown rot and silver leaf. They are also attacked by aphids, red spider and caterpillars. Frost will kill the blossom. For leaf curl, spray with Bordeaux mixture at leaf drop and again at bud burst. At leaf drop clear up the leaves and burn them. For aphids use Dimethoate and for red spider mite Dicofol.

Raspberries
These do not travel well, so if you want fresh raspberries grow your own, and you should get top quality fruit. But first a word of warning: they are subject to virus, so buy canes that are certified virus-free. A position in full sun is best, and if the site has any perennial weeds, eradicate them first or the crop will suffer and get worse as time goes on. All raspberries need a slightly acid soil and in

chalky areas the plant can be seriously affected by iron and manganese deficiency. A well-drained soil is best, and sandy soil will need plenty of humus dug in, as raspberries need a plentiful supply of water in the growing season. After planting, lay a mulch of well-rotted manure, mushroom compost or even straw if none of the others is available, and add to that 1oz of sulphate of ammonia, 1oz of superphosphate and 1oz of sulphate of potash mixed together, to each square yard. Planting the canes can be done in open ground or against a fence.

If in open ground, posts should be put up and wires strung between them to support the canes, and the rows should be 4 – 5 feet apart. Early autumn is the best time for planting, but can be done at any time until spring, providing the soil is dry enough to work well and free from frost. If the canes are bought beforehand, heel them in on spare ground and keep damp until all is ready. The roots should be covered by no more than three inches of soil, and gentle foot pressure applied. In spring, cut back the cane to a live bud about ten inches above soil level. Weeding and watering need to be carried out through the year. If mulched as they should be, few weeds will grow, but the plot will need protecting from birds by netting. Aphids are carriers of virus and should be controlled by spraying.

All the raspberry varieties mentioned here have been raised in Kent at East Malling's Institute of Horticultural Research, and grow well except in chalky areas: Malling Promise (early), Malling Jewel or Malling Delight (mid season), Malling Leo (late) and Malling Bliss (very late).

'Peel me another Hamburg grape Hilda.'

Chapter Fifteen

Grapes — Indoors and Out

Grapes have been grown in Kent since Roman times, and in recent years a number of commercial vineyards have been successfully established in the county. Most gardens have space for this fruitful crop, either along a sheltered wall or inside an unheated greenhouse.

Plant in November or December according to the weather, but never in frosty soil. Outside, a situation on a south or south west wall is best.

Soil preparation

This should be free draining and at least nine inches deep. Add well-rotted farmyard manure or compost to the area, together with 3 – 4oz of ground chalk and 4oz of Growmore.

Dig out the hole to receive the root, and spread the roots in it. Do not plant deeper than it was in the container. After planting, mulch all round with well-rotted farmyard manure or compost to a depth of 4 inches.

Never plant a vine closer to a wall than 9 inches, and if planting in a greenhouse, consider placing the root outside as this will reduce the need for watering. It is advisable at this time either to fix a trellis to the wall, or put wires on vine eyes to support the rod.

It takes three years for the vine to produce properly, and all flowers and fruit should be picked off for the first two.

Training the vine

Remove all long shoots not needed for extra length of the main rod to within two leaves from it. Winter pruning will be done the same way as soon as the leaves have fallen. Do not prune too late in winter as the sap rises early and the vine will bleed. If this happens use talcum powder on the cut.

Feeding

As soon as the leaves appear, feed 2oz of Phostrogen or the equivalent of Tomorite once a week. As soon as the flowers appear, double the amount of feed right up to picking time, and water copiously every day. When fruit forms, reduce the bunches to one per foot if required as dessert grapes, or two for wine making.

Spray with BENLATE once a week throughout the season to stop mildew and botrytis.

Suitable varieties:

Greenhouse
Buckland Sweetwater. Early and quick to mature, suitable for an unheated greenhouse.

Black Hamburgh. The best flavour and most widely grown, sets freely and can be ripened in a cold greenhouse.

Frontignan. Both black and white varieties are early maturing and can be grown in pots under glass.

Foster's Seedling. The best of the sweetwater grapes, sets freely and ripens early. Will do well in a cold greenhouse.

Outside on walls or fences
Muller Thurgau. A Riesling, mid-season, most widely planted. Mid October.

Brant. A hybrid of Canadian origin, heavy crops of small sweet grapes, vigorous. Some resistance to mildew and a useful wall covering.

Cascade. Mid season, resistant to mildew, low in sugar and high in acid, makes a fair quality wine, very vigorous, good as a wall covering.

Muscat Bleu. Excellent flavour dessert grape, large seeds, best on a wall but will ripen in the open in a warm summer. Mid October.

Further information can be found in the Wisley Handbook, 'Grapes', published by the Royal Horticulcural Society.

Chapter Sixteen

Success with Climbers

Clematis

This very popular wall plant is easy to grow and maintain. The general rule for planting all varieties of clematis is 'head in the sun and feet in the cool'. After planting, the area around the root should be covered either with tiles or a large flat stone.

Pruning

Three methods depending on the type:

1. The kinds that can be cut to the ground level or one metre where extra growth is needed include Clematis flammula, C. rehderiana, C. tangutica, C. viticella, and the hybrids Duchess of Albany, Lady Betty Balfour, Perle d'Azur and Royal Velours.
2. Cut out dead wood and shorten to four feet. These include the large flowered hybrids Duchess of Edinburgh, Lasurstern, Miss Bateman, Mrs Cholmondeley, Nelly Moser and Vyvyan Pennell.
3. Remove only dead wood or prune if space is limited: C. alpina, C. amandii, C. chrysocoma, C. montana, and C. macropetala.

All pruning to be done February – March weather permitting, and not in frosty conditions.

Feeding

Add humus at planting time. This can be farmyard manure, composted chicken droppings, mushroom compost, or your own compost to which a general fertilizer should be added. Feed the plants each year with 4oz of Growmore to each, plus a handful of Epsom salts early in March.

Repeat at the end of May, and ensure the plants are well watered from then on, as most clematis are planted against walls. They tend to dry out faster in such places than if planted by a pergola or over a tree.

Pests

Not much attacks clematis, but slugs can be a problem in the early stages, and slug killer around the plant is a wise precaution.

Earwigs eating the leaves and flowers can be cleared up by spraying with Sybol.

Disease

By far the worst thing that can happen to clematis is WILT. But all is not lost even then, as only the shoots are affected. The treatment is simple: remove the soil around the plant to expose the crown, cut off all the wilted material, and flood the area with BENLATE. Back-fill with fresh soil, and flood that also with the rest of the Benlate.

Replace the tiles or stones to keep the root cool.

Powdery Mildew. This can be treated with a fungicide such as Multirose.

Propagation

In the early days clematis were grafted on the stocks of wild clematis, the old man's beard of the hedgerow. Nowadays cuttings can be taken of all varieties except C. texensis and this could be difficult.

The cuttings are best taken from the middle of June until the last week in July.

If you are growing them outside, find a sheltered spot out of direct sunshine, and if inside the greenhouse, put them on the floor under the bench, and keep damp at all times. Heavy shading must be used for the first month and then light can be increased.

For one or more cuttings, prepare a pot of 50 – 50 peat and sharp sand, or use a five-inch half pot and place your cuttings around the edge, two inches apart. Dust the top of the pot with sulphur.

To be successful the cuttings must be from one year old wood, not new tips. Select your material from the growing plant, and in order to distinguish the year-old wood it will be brown in colour.

With a sharp knife or razor blade, cut one inch above the two leaves and three inches below it.

Cut one leaf off and holding the cutting, take a thin slice off the 3-inch side, 1½ inches long.

All cuttings should then be dipped in Captan solution, shaken off and the tip dipped in rooting compound.

The cutting should then be pushed into the pot and firmed to exclude air from around the stem. The buds should just rest on the surface of the compost. They will stay in their position until next February or March, and if rooted well, potted on or planted out in their final position.

Stand them on a gravel bed, and take off any dead leaf or debris as this will stop light getting to them.

Growing from seed

Only C. tangutica, C. orientalis and C. flammula will come true from seed, and some of that is erratic, sometimes taking a year to germinate. C. tangutica is easy: when the head is ripe and dry, cut off the feather and break up the seed head. Plant ⅛ inch deep in a peat based compost, and stand it on the kitchen windowsill or in the greenhouse. Prick into 3-inch pots when large enough to handle and stand them in a frame. They can flower in a year if planted as soon as they are a foot high, and will grow in a northern or eastern position.

Campsis radicans
A genus of two species of climbers known by the common name Trumpet Vine. Most of the varieties can only be grown in a greenhouse, and all need some support as they climb by twining.

The best variety is Campsis 'Madam Galen' which is hardier than the rest and will grow well on a south wall in well cultivated soil. But protect from frost in the first year.

Propagation is by layering or by root cuttings taken in autumn and given bottom heat. Seed can also be used, but needs stratification and is not easy.

Pruning
This is done in February and if it has been a hard winter the plant should be cut back drastically.

Eccremocarpus
Known as the Chilean Glory Flower, of which three varieties are grown in Kent. E. scaber is the most common with orange flowers, E. aureus is the yellow variety, and E. rubra the red. This is more tender than the others. Although they are all half hardy, they will stand a mild winter. If cut down by frost and the crown of the plant is covered with chipped bark it will survive. They need strong supports against a wall, but will climb over pergolas and fences. They can be invasive, but do not mind being tipped. Each flower sets a seed pod in which there can be 80 – 100 seeds, and most of it will grow in the soil in Kent, even after a hard winter.

If you buy or get seed from a neighbour, sow in April, weather permitting, or in pots in the greenhouse, and plant out when large enough. It will grow in an eastern or northern position in the southern counties, and if allowed to scramble over shrubs they will come to no harm as the foliage is soft. Eccremocarpus will grow on most soils, even in the cracks of paths.

Honeysuckle
Some are climbers and one or two are the shrub variety, but these appear only to grow in larger gardens. It is native to western Europe and will do better in full sun than in partial shade. It will not tolerate dry conditions, but will stand low temperatures. The climbing

varieties need a robust trellis or pergola for support, and one frequently seen is the evergreen L. nitida used as a hedge. That again needs a strong support. L. pileata is very often used as ground cover but the best of the climbers are L. fragrantissima that flowers in January with cream flowers, and L. tatarica that blooms in June with pink flowers, or go for 'Baggesen's Gold' the yellow leaved variety.

Lonicera is generally propagated by layering, and if this cannot be done in the soil beneath the plant, hang up a pot and layer in that, but keep it damp. When planting, choose a sunny spot and dig in plenty of humus and a handful of bonemeal. If against a wall line the hole between the plant roots and the wall with a small sheet of polythene, as water will be taken by the wall.

Pests in the form of greenfly are easily dealt with by sprays, but earwigs do eat the leaf and these can be caught in inverted flower pots filled with straw and shaken into a bucket of water with paraffin in it.

Feed at least twice a year, and water in dry weather, and they will reward you with their delightful scent.

Ivies

If it is colour in winter or green in summer you want, and a plant that will grow anywhere on walls, fences or trees, and is very hardy coming from Europe and Asia, ivies are the ones to go for, but as with all other climbing plants, they need regular pruning to ease the weight from walls and keep them tidy. There are fifteen varieties in the wild, and eight cultivated kinds. Three of them are variegated: Hedera Goldheart, H. canariensis 'Variegata' and H. colchica 'Dentata'. A good, large, green-leaved ivy is H. colchica.

Plant the variegated types where they will get some sun. Any soil will do, even the heavy clays, and in very dry periods no watering is necessary. All ivies can be used as ground cover and on a steep bank, planted at the top to grow down. Nothing is better, and although it was used in the past as a medicinal plant (as the leaf contains hederin), it is generally considered to be poisonous.

Nasturtiums (Tropaeolum)

As a summer fill-in, where you are going to put a permanent plant later on, try the climbing nasturtium. As they come in various forms, some for climbing, trailing and short ones for the border, be sure to check the seed packet. You will need either pea sticks or trellis up the wall and they can go to six feet. Do not manure, as they prefer a poor, free-draining soil, and water in dry weather is the only thing they will need. Sow the seeds in February or April where they will flower and, if the weather is bad, sow under glass or even indoors on the kitchen window sill, and plant out when large enough.

Two climbers to look for: 'Tall Mixed' or 'Climbing Mixed' and the colours include red, yellow and orange. Or go for the yellow Canary Creeper (T. peregrinum). This one will need a better manured soil and is a vigorous climber with small blooms and lobed leaves. Again it must have support. Blackfly can be troublesome so a spray is called for. The seeds have been used in the past as capers, pickled in vinegar.

Climbing roses

Whether on the side of a cottage or over a trellis, a climbing rose is always a thing of beauty. There are many varieties from which to choose, of which the following are just a few:

Highfield Mimosa (yellow and fragrant), Albertine (salmon and fragrant), Dorothy Perkins (rose pink and free-flowering), Paul's Scarlet (bright scarlet and large flowered), and Longicuspis (white and very rampant — ideal to grow in a tree). Planting can be done from February to March and the soil should be built up first with well-rotted dung. If using your own compost, add a general fertilizer to it. Mulching early in the season with dung, compost or forest bark will help the plant to survive through the dry months, and slug pellets under the mulch will deter these pests. Watering will always be necessary on light soils.

Pruning

In September cut out the old wood from early flowering climbers, and tie back the new wood in a fan shape to encourage new shoots. All late climbers to be pruned as above but in March.

Ramblers, as opposed to climbing roses: merely cut out the old wood and tip back the laterals that have flowered.

In late March or April, according to the weather, apply fertilizer around the plants and work lightly into the soil. A foliar feed is advisable in May, especially on light soils. In June apply fertilizer again to the soil around the plant, and this will be the last until the following year.

Look out for greenfly, caterpillars, black spot, mildew and rust all through the year and use the appropriate sprays.

In October – November make sure all ties are in place and give the plants a clean up, not forgetting to clear dead leaves from around the base.

Passion Flower (Passiflora)
If you live in a frost pocket this climber is not for you. P. caerulea is
the most widely grown in this country, but a severe winter will kill
the top growth, although if the root is covered it should survive. It
may be planted in good garden soil, preferably near a south or south-
west wall, and a trellis is needed as the plant climbs with the aid of
tendrils. In a good year it can go to twenty feet. The flowers appear
between June and September and have a religious significance. In a
good year they will produce seed pods about two inches long which
are not edible. The seed can be saved and sown in spring under glass.
Cuttings root very easily. Take them six inches long and put in a
propagator with bottom heat from May to September or layer shoots
in summer.

There is a white variety (Constance Elliott) but the seed is hard to
come by. Treatment is the same.

Russian Vine (Polygonum baldschuanicum)
Some like it, some do not, but for covering dead trees and sheds it is
the fastest growing plant of its kind and is not known as the mile a
minute plant for nothing. Any soil will do, and you do not have to
worry about sun or shade — it grows in either. To increase your
plant stock, put cuttings in the cold frame in summer. Its only
disadvantage is that it loses its leaves in winter, and pruning can be
heavy in spring. Some support is necessary.

Virginia Creeper (Parthenocissus)
This climber's beauty is seen in autumn if you grow the P.
quinquefolia with its red leaves covering the walls, and is the best
known in this country. There is also the variegated P. henryana — a
good plant for a north wall. In all there are fifteen species of this
plant, and they all need something to start them climbing. Later they
will climb with the aid of suckers on the end of their tendrils. They
will climb trees, but look better against a wall.

Any good garden soil will do, and they should be trimmed in
spring to remove any unwanted growth.

When leaves fall they should be composted on their own, as they
rot at a slower rate than most greenstuff on the compost heap.

Wistaria
The king of the climbers, but with a little care it can also be grown as
a weeping standard. There are ten species of this beautiful plant, but
the most widely grown is the Wistaria floribunda with flowers of
violet and violet-blue. There is also a white floribunda 'Alba', and

the double white Wistaria venusta. They will grow on any ordinary well-drained soil, and a sunny sheltered position such as a south or south west facing wall is essential.

Wiring the wall or fixing a trellis to provide a permanent support must be done from the onset of planting, as there is considerable weight in a full grown plant.

Planting.

Do this between October and March, and give it plenty of root space. The roots should not damage the footings of the house. Having dug the hole, mix bonemeal in the soil at the bottom. Water for a while after planting to get the plant established, and do not expect it to flower for at least five years. Avoid high nitrogen feeds as these will only result in green growth and few flowers. Use a high potash fertilizer such as used for roses or tomatoes.

Pruning.

This is done in two stages: in July the long growths are cut back to within six leaves of the base, except where needed to increase the plant. In February cut back again to 2 – 3 buds from the base to encourage formation of flowering spurs.

Pests and diseases

Aphids and thrips can be dealt with by spraying. Birds sometimes tend to peck off flowers but in larger plants this will usually not be noticed. Some plants are attacked by Leaf Spot. This is a fungal disease and should be treated with a fungicide.

Chapter Seventeen

Growing Plants for Kentish Beds and Borders
(Annuals and Perennials)

Summer bedding plants

Although bedding plants can be bought all ready for putting out, owners of frost-free greenhouses can easily raise their own from seed at a fraction of the cost. Most of the extra equipment can be used year after year, and the outlay will soon be repaid. There is also the advantage of growing a far wider range of varieties than is available in most shops or garden centres.

Choice of seed

Most plants grown for summer bedding are what are known as half hardy annuals; too tender to stand our Kentish winters but will flourish once all fear of frost has passed. Seed catalogues offer a vast selection of suitable plants, and are a mine of useful information. Some of the most popular bedding plants grown from seed include the following which all do well in the county of Kent:

Ageratum: mainly blue and around 8 inches tall. A good edging plant as well as for general bedding.

Alyssum: popular dwarf plants for low edging. Usually white, but lilac-pink, purple and violet are also available.

Antirrhinum: various heights from 6 inches to 3 feet, these popular 'Snapdragons' range in colour through white, yellow, orange, red and pink, together with mixtures.

Asters: flower from late summer to autumn and vary in height from 6 inches to 2 feet. Colours include white, pink, red, and mauve, and there are single and double forms.

Begonias: these are the fibrous-rooted form (Semperflorens) and have a long flowering period from July to October. They perform well in a wet season and also in dry conditions if some water is provided. Height is about 8 inches and colours are mainly red, pink and white. There are both green and bronze foliage kinds.

Cineraria maritima: grown for its attractive, bright silver foliage, this plant makes an excellent foil for many others and thrives in dry conditions. Height is 9 – 12 inches.

Cosmos: an upstanding, bright plant with attractive fern-like foliage and masses of single dahlia-like flowers in crimson, rose or white and is also good for cutting.

'Bad news dear, slugs approaching the Delphiniums.'

Gazania: less common than some bedding plants, their attractive and unusual flowers thrive in bright sunshine. Height around 12 inches.

Impatiens: the much loved Busy Lizzies. They grow and flower splendidly in cool and shady places which are often difficult, but also do well in bright sun. Colours range from white through brilliant rose and red to softer hues of mauve. Height 6 – 8 inches. They also make useful pot plants.

Lobelia: trailing forms are a must for hanging baskets and the upright kinds make superb edging for beds and borders. Colours range from light blue to mauve and dark blue, as well as white.

Marigolds, African: reliable, trouble-free plants which give a blaze of colour from July until the first frosts of autumn. Heights range from around 12 inches to 2 feet. Colours yellow and orange and mixtures.

Marigolds, French: easy to grow and quick to flower, they need a sunny position and their display will last from June until autumn if regular dead heading is done. Height around 8 – 12 inches. Single and double kinds are available in a range of orange, yellow and mahogany red.

Mimulus: once regarded mainly as a bog plant, modern strains of the popular 'Monkey Flower' do well in most situations, providing the soil is fairly moist. They will also do well in window boxes and hanging baskets.

Nemesia: one of the widest range of colours among bedding plants and around 9 inches high, they are a useful filler in bedding schemes.

Nicotiana: these smaller relations of the tobacco plant have upward-facing flowers which continue throughout the season. Scented varieties are a delight on summer evenings. Height about 12 inches.

Petunias: colourful plants with large, single or double flowers in a wide range of colours including white, pink, red, blue and mauve. Very suitable for baskets and other containers as well as bedding. Height 9 – 12 inches.

Phlox drummondii: dwarf, bushy plants covered in flowers ranging from pink through red to violet. 6 – 12 inches high.

Salvia splendens: Sturdy plants flowering from July onwards. Vivid scarlet blooms are eye-catching, and there are now pink, white and purple strains. About 12 inches high.

Stocks: single and double fragrant flowers in mauve, red, pink and white on sturdy stems. 12 – 24 inches high.

Tagetes: reliable, bushy plants for edging and bedding. Like a small French marigold. Long-lasting flowers of yellow or orange on 9-inch high stems.

Verbena: colourful plants for bedding, edging and window boxes. Flowers of purple, red and white, sometimes with an eye. Most kinds are about 8 inches tall. Long flowering period from June to October.

Sowing the seeds

With the smaller number of seeds in most packets these days, half or even quarter size seed trays offer ample space for most sowings. Cheap and nasty trays are a false economy as they soon become brittle and split. Thicker plastic trays are more expensive, but last for many years if carefully cleaned after use and properly stored. Use a good compost; either a multipurpose peat-based kind or John Innes seed compost. This contains phosphate to stimulate growth of the tiny seedlings' roots. Always sow the seeds as evenly and thinly as possible. This is easy with the larger kinds, but very fine, dust-like seeds such as begonia are best mixed first with a small quantity of dry, fine silver sand. This makes it easy to achieve a good, even coverage over the whole area. Take care to observe the seedsmen's recommendations regarding covering the seeds. As a general rule the seeds should be given a covering of sifted compost equal to their diameter, but certain seeds need light to germinate and should merely be pressed into the surface. Finally, stand the filled seed tray in an inch of water, and leave there until the surface of the compost starts to glisten.

Germinating

Recommended temperatures for germination vary, but are mainly between 65 – 75°F and generally not critical. A heated greenhouse propagator is needed if many sowings are made, but a warm place such as the airing cupboard can often serve well in the early stages. Cover seed trays with glass before putting in the propagator, and turn it every day to avoid drips of water falling on the seedlings as they emerge. This could be a cause of damping-off disease. Remove the glass entirely before the growing seedlings reach it. Give the trays plenty of light in the early stages, but shade from direct sun as this can scorch the tender young plants.

Pricking out

As soon as the seedlings are large enough to handle, they should be replanted in larger trays, spacing them about two inches apart each way. Keep the trays well watered with a fine rose on a watering can.

Hardening off

Once the plants are well established in their trays, transfer them to the cold frame so they gradually become accustomed to outside temperatures. Ventilate during the daytime, but close the frame at night as long as frosts are likely.

Planting out
The areas to be planted should be watered well the day beforehand, and the young plants set in firmly, using a trowel. Check the seedsmen's recommended spacings and plant accordingly, watering afterwards to settle the soil well around the roots.

Aftercare
Planting out time for bedding plants often coincides with a dry spell and further watering should be given before the plants show signs of wilting. This should be followed by regular liquid feeding to ensure healthy, vigorous growth and a colourful display. As the first flush of flowers fades, take care to remove the old blooms to prevent them setting seed. If this is carried out, a colourful show will often continue until the first frosts arrive.

Hardy Annuals
As their name implies, these 'tougher' plants grow, flower, seed and die-off in one year, but can survive the rigours of our Kentish winters outside. They are usually sown in their final flowering positions, in areas marked out beforehand with outlines of dry sand to guide the sowing. This is best done in straight rows or drills within these 'drifts', as this makes it easier to recognise the young plants when weeding. And there is plenty of that! An annual bed or border prepared in this way can be a fairly cheap but colourful feature of any garden, as long as care is taken to get the plant heights right when sowing. Tall plants at the front can soon screen their shorter companions. Such a display is also demanding of much dead-heading at flowering time and in a poor season the results can be disastrous. We prefer to raise the hardy annuals in much the same way as the half-hardy plants above, but the temperatures needed are much less of course.

A selection of hardy annuals we have found do well in the county:

Anchusa: compact, 9-inch plants with pink, lavender, blue and white flowers. Attractive to bees.

Bartonia: worthwhile, though not commonly seen. Glistening yellow flowers on 18-inch plants which bloom all summer.

Calendula (pot marigold): colours range from cream to tangerine. Prolifically flowering spreading plants from 1 – 2 feet high.

Candytuft: neat plants with white, pink and red flowers. Good for edging, 8 inches.

Chrysanthemum (annual): brightly coloured, daisy-type flowers of yellow, red and bronze. Good for cutting. Plants grow 1½ – 2 feet high.

Clarkia: red, pink and white flowers clustered on graceful stems. Grow 1 – 2 feet high.

Cornflower: both tall and short varieties of this well-known flower — and pink, red and white as well as the original blue can be obtained. Taller kinds may need some support.

Dimorphotheca (Osteospermum, Star of the Veldt): for a sunny spot. Low-growing, with white, yellow and orange flowers.

Echium: bushy, long-lasting plants with blue, pink and white flowers. 12 inches high.

Eschscholzia (sic!) (Californian poppy): brilliant red, pink, orange and yellow flowers, even in poor, dry soil. Needs a sunny spot (1 foot high).

Gypsophila (annual): dainty sprays of white flowers ideal for mixing with cut blooms, especially sweet peas. 18 inches high.

Godetia: free-flowering, bushy plants with red, pink and white flowers over a long season. 15 inches high.

Larkspur: blue, pink, purple or white flowers on tall stems, useful for cutting. 2 – 4 feet high.

Lavatera: bushy plants for the back of border. Striking display of white or pink trumpet-shaped flowers which lasts from midsummer to late autumn. 2 – 3 feet high.

Nasturtium: will do well in hot, dry places and on poor soil. Colours include yellow, orange and red. There are single and double forms for edging, hanging baskets and covering trellis, as well as for bedding.

Nemesia: bushy plants 9 inches high with a wide range of flower colour. Useful for bedding.

Nemophila (Baby Blue Eyes): easily grown carpeting annual with sky-blue flowers.

Nigella (Love in a Mist): delicate, feathery foliage with blue, white or pink flowers. 18 inches high.

Sunflower: easy to grow. Large, yellow flowers on tall stems. Seeds can be eaten or fed to parrots.

Sweet pea: although often grown in their own right as a flower for cutting, they are excellent up trellises and the dwarf forms can rampage over beds. Wide range of colours, some are scented.

Viscaria: showy and easily grown, they like the sun. Blue, pink and red mixture, 10 – 15 inches high.

Virginian stock: early, dwarf and free-flowering, pink and white flowers.

There are plenty more! Browse through the seed catalogues and take your pick.

Herbaceous perennials

These more permanent plants deserve a place in any garden scheme. With a measure of maintenance they can give a long-lasting, colourful display, not only in beds and borders, but in odd corners, too.

Always prepare the ground well beforehand, as these welcome guests will hopefully be staying some time. Clear away all perennial weeds, cultivate well, and incorporate lots of bulky organic matter and some bonemeal.

Many attractive plants are available, and a good selection can be made from the following list:

Achillea (Yarrow): 1 – 5 feet, flat yellow heads in early to late summer with fern-like foliage.

Alchemilla mollis: 18 inches. Sprays of yellow flowers, pretty leaves.

Alstroemeria (Peruvian Lily) Ligtu Hybrid: 2 – 3 feet, range of colours, deep rich soil in the sun. Takes time to become established.

Anemone japonica: 3 feet, white, pink and mauve, tolerates shade and flowers in late summer.

Aquilegia (Columbine, Granny's Bonnet): 18 – 30 inches. Graceful spurred pastel-coloured flowers in early summer.

Aster (Michaelmas Daisy): 6 inches to 6 feet! Wide variety available. Late summer/autumn flowering.

Campanula (Bell Flowers): 3 feet, several suitable species with blue or white flowers.

Chrysanthemum Maximum (Shasta Daisy): 2 – 3 feet, white flowers on long stems from July to September.

Delphinium: 5 – 7 feet, imposing spikes of mainly white and blue flowers (but also, lately, red) which need staking. Deep rich soil in sun. Beware of slugs!

Dianthus (border carnations and pinks): 6 – 12 inches. Red, pink and white. Like lime and are good by the sea.

Doronicum (Leopard's Bane): 2 feet. Large golden daisies in April, useful early flowering plant in the border.

Echinops (Globe Thistle): striking blue-grey spherical spiky flowers in mid to late summer. Much used by flower arrangers.

Erigeron (Fleabane): 2 feet. Like a large-flowered Michaelmas Daisy, flowers June – October.

Euphorbia (Spurges): wide selection of different types. Unusual and striking plants e.g. E. griffithii (Fireglow).

Gaillardia (Blanket Flower): 3 feet. Showy yellow or orange daisy type flowers which need some staking.

Geraniums (Cranesbill): 18 – 30 inches. Bushy plants make good, spreading ground cover. Flowers mainly blue or mauve. Several species.

Geum (Avens): 1 – 2 feet. Forms dense clumps with red or yellow flowers. Good for cutting. Long flowering period.

Gypsophila (Baby's Breath): 2 feet. Dainty sprays of small white or pink flowers. Likes lime. Flowers June – August.

Helenium (Sneezewort): 3 – 4 feet. Bronze or yellow showy flowers over a long season.

Hellebores (Christmas and Lenten Roses): 12 – 18 inches. Striking, winter-flowering plants for shady places.

Hemerocallis (Day Lily): 2 – 3 feet. Flowers of many colours, each lasting one day and produced from June – August.

Heuchera (Coral Flower): 12 – 18 inches. Graceful sprays of red or pink flowers from June – September.

Hosta (Plantain Lily): 18 – 30 inches. Attractive, mainly large leaves, suitable for shady, damp situations.

Iris: 9 – 30 inches. Very large range of attractive different kinds of these sun-loving plants to suit many types of location.

Kniphofia (Red Hot Poker): 2 – 4 feet. Striking large spikes of red, yellow or white flowers on long stems from June – October. Needs sun.

Lupinus (Lupin): 3 – 4 feet. Well-known favourite plant with striking spikes of brightly coloured flowers. Dislikes limey soils.

Lysimachia (Loosestrife): 2 – 3 feet. Whorls of bright yellow flowers from June to August.

Nepeta (Catmint): 18 inches. Bushy plants with lavender-purple flowers from May – September and a magnet to all cats in the vicinity.

Oenothera (Evening Primrose): 6 – 18 inches according to type. Striking large flowers which open in evenings. Prefers light soil and sun.

Paeonia (Peony): 2 feet. Large, red, pink or white blooms in midsummer. Gross feeders.

Papaver (Oriental Poppy): 3 feet. White, pink, orange and red striking, bowl-shaped flowers with black centres in May and June. Messy after flowering so needs screening by other planting.

Phlox: 2 – 4 feet. Wide range of colours from white to purple in late summer. Plant them deeply in shaded, rich soil.

Pulmonaria (Lungwort): 1 foot. Pink flowers turning to blue in late spring with striking spotted leaves. Shade is tolerated. Moist position preferred.

Rudbeckia (Coneflower): 2 – 3 feet. Daisy-like yellow orange flowers with protruding centres late summer/autumn.

Scabiosa (Scabious): 2 – 3 feet. Attractive blue, mauve or white flowers on long stems from June to October. Unsuitable for acid soils.

Sedum (Stonecrop, Ice Plant): 1 – 2 feet. Large pink or red flower heads in late summer. Very attractive to butterflies. Fleshy leaves. Happy in hot and dry conditions.

Solidago (Golden Rod): 1 – 6 feet. Yellow flowers in August. Modern hybrids, much less rampant than older and often much-abused kinds.

Stachys (Lamb's Ears): 18 inches. Grown mainly for attractive felted silvery foliage.

Verbascum (Mullein): 3 – 6 feet. Striking mainly yellow spikes of flowers in summer with attractive felted silver leaves.

Local colour!

Some different plants with Kentish names for you to find and plant:

Abutilon, Ashford Red and Kentish Belle
Azalea, Medway
Campanula carpatica, Ditton Blue
Canterbury Bells
Fuchsia, Kentish Belle
Iris, Kent Pride
Narcissus, Clare Park and Narcissus Larkfield
Origanum, Kent Beauty and Kent Pride
Rose, Sissinghurst Castle
Rosemary, Benenden Blue, and Sissinghurst
Rubus X tridel, Benenden
Verbena, Sissinghurst
Viola, Sissinghurst and Swanley White

'I was looking for greenfly.'

Chapter Eighteen

Making a Bottle Garden

A collection of plants in a large glass bottle can be a constant source of interest indoors, and needs very little attention once established. Although the traditional glass carboys in which acid and distilled water were once supplied are very hard to come by, rather smaller, specially-made bottles are generally available and can look most effective when properly planted. These newer containers have quite a large neck, but those lucky enough to acquire a traditional carboy will need to make a few special tools for reaching inside the narrower opening to do the work. Bamboo canes about 2 feet long are used as handles, and to the end of one is taped an old teaspoon for use as a trowel, to another a dinner fork, and a piece of bent wire to hold the plants' roots is fixed to the third. The fourth has a cotton reel pushed on to its end for firming the compost inside the bottle as planting is done.

Start by making sure the container is clean and thoroughly dry, and then put some drainage material in the bottom. This can be plain gravel or one of the manufactured porous clay 'pebbles' which are widely available today. Use a simple funnel made from a circle of thin card with a segment removed, and pour in enough of the pebbles to make a layer about an inch thick. Follow this with a 2 – 3-inch layer of a good, peat-based potting compost to which a handful of crushed lump charcoal has been added to keep it 'sweet'. This growing area will be far more interesting if shaped to various contours instead of being quite flat. A few stones will also add extra character when the planting is done — but do insert them with care! Then water the compost evenly without wetting the sides of the jar. This can be tricky, and is best done with a small funnel fixed to a length of plastic tubing to reach down near the compost.

Choice of plants

These should all be slow-growing, non-flowering, moisture-loving plants. A selection might include small specimens of the following: ferns such as the pteris, Maranta (the Prayer Plant), Peperomia, Pilea (the Aluminium Plant), Saxifraga sarmentosa (Mother of Thousands) and small-leaved ivies.

Decide first where the plants are going, and then make a hollow with the spoon, insert a plant and firm down gently with the cotton reel rammer. When planting is finished, insert a cork in the top to retain moisture. Bottle gardens do best in good light but away from the rays of the sun. If the inside of the glass mists over after a while, remove the cork until all is clear, and then replace it. Further watering is rarely necessary.

Old fish tanks or goldfish bowls also make useful and effective containers for planting in the same way, and can be sealed by covering with glass or plastic film.

Chapter Nineteen

The Care of Some Popular House Plants

African Violets

One of our most popular pot plants, being perfectly at home on a window sill where it has good light. The compost should be kept moist but only watered when the plant is 'begging for water'. Use tepid water and keep it off the leaves and central crown. Avoid wide variations of temperature and aim for a minimum of 60°F. A humid atmosphere is essential, and the plants should be stood on a tray of moist pebbles if air in the room is very dry.

Amaryllis

More properly called the Hippeastrum, the plant should be fed either with Phostrogen or Tomorite from the start of growth, a third of the recommended feed should be given at every watering. When flowering has finished, the flower and stalk should be cut off. If the tips of the plant are going brown, lay the pot on its side in a frost-free place such as the bottom of the greenhouse or shed until completely dried out. As this happens, remove the bulb from the pot, clean up and store in a PAPER bag until next August or September and then plant in fresh compost.

Aspidistra

The aspidistra is known as the Cast Iron plant for good reason. It thrives on neglect and has been known to grow in the same position and pot for 14 years. It was a Victorian favourite because of its ability to withstand draughts and shade. It will also tolerate much dryness if the temperature is not too high.

Aspidistras dislike over-watering or frequent repotting. Do not feed, as this will cause brown patches to appear on the leaves. There are two varieties: the old Aspidistra elatior which has been in this country for many years, and a comparative newcomer, Aspidistra elatior 'Variegata'. This is more attractive with cream-striped leaves but is not so hardy. Wash aspidistra leaves occasionally with tepid water and a soft sponge, keep out of direct sunlight, and you will have the plant for years.

'Come on, I promise I'll never leave you again.'

Azaleas

Many indoor azaleas are bought each year at Christmas, and the usual type is the Indian azalea. When buying, pick one with few flowers and lots of buds, and before taking it out of the shop or garden centre, have it wrapped; a sudden change of temperature will make it lose its leaves and flowers. The plant should be kept damp but not wet, and in a cool and brightly-lit situation, but away from direct sunlight, 50 – 60°F is ideal. Always use soft water as azaleas are lime-hating plants. If your water is chalky, boil first and allow to cool — or use rain water. When flowering has finished, and after all danger of frost has passed, the plant can be put in the garden in a shady place for the summer months, and kept damp. Remember to bring it inside again before the frosts return. An occasional feed of Sequestered Iron with Feed will keep the plant in good order, and when repotting use Ericaceous compost. Three common kinds are Rhododendron simsii, R. obtusum and R. obtusum 'Coral Bells'.

Christmas and Easter Cacti

These are forest cacti as opposed to the desert kind, and as such need different treatment. The Rat Tail Cactus is related, but should be treated in the same way as desert cacti. They are Epiphyllums and in their natural environment they live in trees.

Both plants are reluctant to flower unless certain rules are followed: never move the plants when in bud or flower, and give them a summer outside to bake the joints of the leaves. At the end of the summer, take off the first 1 – 2 inches of compost and replace with fresh cactus compost. Do not repot completely as the plant has to be pot bound to flower.

Return plants to the house well before the first frosts, and put in a cool place at an average of 50 – 55°F. After Christmas, mist the plants to start them off, and a fortnight later water lightly and increase this as the buds come.

Give a small feed or two while the plant is budding and flowering.

Choose a well lit spot for it to flower, out of sunlight, preferably in an east window.

Use rain water as much as possible, as our Kentish tap water is too hard. Water liberally in the flowering period.

Cuttings of both varieties are easy: take off the terminal tip and allow to dry out for 2 – 3 days. Then plant in a peat-based compost, and keep damp and out of sunlight.

The Christmas Cactus is Schlumbergera truncata, and the Easter Cactus is Schlumbergera gaertneri.

Chlorophytum

This is the popular Spider Plant, so called after the young plantlets which are borne on its long white stems. It will tolerate most light conditions, but should preferably be away from direct sunlight. Aim for a winter minimum of 45°F and repot in spring if needed.

Feed regularly and water well in spring, summer and autumn, but give only a little in winter.

Clivia Miniata (The Kaffir Lily)

This plant is not as easy to grow as many house plants, but succeeds if conditions are right. It needs plenty of room, no feeding, an unheated room, the minimum of water and a resting period through the winter. Avoid moving the plant when in flower, and never repot unless absolutely necessary, when it should be done after flowering.

Temperature 40 – 50°F no more, in winter, good light, but avoid direct sun. Water very little in winter. Most of the Clivia have orange flowers but there are also red, yellow and cream varieties.

After flowering, if no seed has set, the flower stalk should be cut off. If seed has set it must be ripe before sowing.

Cyclamen

Sadly, many cyclamen are thrown away after flowering, but with care they can be kept for a number of years. Plant them concave side up, and to half the depth of the corm. Replant in August for flowering in winter, and use soft, tepid water at all times.

In the flowering season they need a temperature of 50 – 60°F and good light, but not bright sunlight. Keep compost damp at all times when flowering. It is a good idea to stand the pot on a saucer of pea gravel, and put water and feed in that.

Most of the problems with cyclamen are caused by heat or not watering. Feeding can be done with any of the balanced feeds, but only in the flowering period.

After flowering, lay the pot on its side in a frost-free place to dry out. Remove the corm from the pot when drying is done, clean it up and store in a paper bag. Around midsummer, repot in new peat-based compost and start off again in a north facing window.

Seed can be sown in late summer in a temperature of 60 – 70°F, and it will take 16 – 18 months to flower.

There are 12 varieties of the larger types of cyclamen (9 – 12 inches tall), and 6 of the miniature varieties (7 inches or less), and all are treated in the same way.

Some miniature varieties are scented; two of the best of these are Puppet and Symphony.

The address of the Cyclamen Society is P. Moore Esq., Tile Barn House, Standen Street, Iden Green, Benenden, Kent, TN17 4LB.

Dieffenbachia or Dumb Cane
Sometimes also known as the Leopard Lily, this attractive foliage plant is harder to grow than some, as it dislikes dry air and cold draughts. An even temperature of about 60°F is preferred in winter when it needs more light than during the summer months. A humid atmosphere should be provided round the plant by standing on a tray of moist pebbles or peat. The sap of this plant can badly affect the mouth, and it should be kept well away from young children.

Ficus Elastica
The good old rubber plant — a favourite of the fifties which bounced back and is still going strong! The variety 'decora' is most common and the plain leaved kinds are generally easier to grow than variegated versions. They will tolerate winter temperatures down to 55°F and are happy with little direct sunlight. Allow the compost to become dry before watering, and give only a little water in winter. When the plant becomes too tall for the room it can be 'air layered' to give a new plant for growing on. Air layering involves removing a circle of bark from the stem, dusting with root powder, and surrounding with damp sphagnum moss enclosed in a polythene bag. This is tied to the stem above and below the cut part, and left for about eight weeks. When roots are seen in the sphagnum moss, the stem can be cut below the tie, the polythene removed and the new plant potted up carefully in good compost.

Hibiscus
A most attractive house plant with glossy, dark green leaves and striking, large red or pink trumpet-shaped flowers. It does best at temperatures between 60 – 77°F and prefers a light situation, even direct sun. Ample watering should be given but must not be allowed to stand in water. Some gentle misting in summer time is also beneficial. Feed once a week during the summer months.

Hoya
The attractive Wax Plant is a favourite indoor climber and will survive a minimum of 50 – 55°F in the winter months when watering should be reduced. Bright light is best but avoid strong summer sunshine.

Poinsettia

Widely given as Christmas presents and often kept growing throughout the following year. Most plants sold have been treated with growth retarding chemicals but subsequent growth is much taller. To ensure the attractive red bracts by Christmas, the plant must have 14 hours total darkness each day for eight weeks from the end of September. An interesting exercise, but better perhaps to start from new each year. A minimum of 55 – 60°F should be maintained and the compost allowed to become dry between waterings.

Streptocarpus

Who has not admired many of the one hundred species of this plant in flower? If you follow the rules, bearing in mind that the plant is sub tropical, you will delight in the blooms it produces. Keep the plants in either an eastern or northern window, and if forced to keep them in a south facing one, keep them from strong sunlight. They like a warm, moist atmosphere in summer, and pots should be stood on a saucer filled with damp pea gravel or grit. This will create the right conditions. Reduce the watering in winter, and keep in not less than 50 – 60°F or the leaves will go grey and brittle. As soon as the small flower buds appear, feeding should begin with one of the general fertilizers. Put a quarter of the feed recommended in every watering throughout the flowering season. Apart from seed, most new streptocarpus plants are grown from leaf cuttings, and there are two ways of achieving this. Take half a leaf, score the rib on the underside and press this into a damp compost, or divide a leaf into two-inch pieces and insert them into a seed tray of 50 – 50 peat and sharp sand compost, base down and one inch in the compost. In both cases they should then be put in a warm place with good light but out of direct sunlight. Pot on into John Innes No.2 if you are going to keep them for more than one year.

Seed can be sown on the surface of a pot containing a peat-based compost in late winter or spring. The pot is then put into a polythene bag and a temperature of 65°F maintained. When large enough to handle, pot on into 3-inch pots or trays, and finally into 5-inch pots.

The most common streptocarpus is 'Constant Nymph', but there are varying shades of pink, blue, purple, violet and white, sometimes with 'pencilling' in the throat of the flower. All have the blooms standing on stalks up to nine inches long.

Chapter Twenty

A Kentish Herb Garden

Although any growing plant without a woody stem is technically speaking 'a herb', the word has mainly come to mean those plants with a use in food, as a medicine, or for cosmetic purposes. In recent years the growing interest in these plants has seen them appearing widely, and herb gardens have become popular features in most planting schemes. Culinary herbs are by far the most commonly cultivated and if growing near the kitchen door can give added zest to most dishes.

Layout of Herb Gardens
Designs can be made to suit almost any space and we have seen fine herb gardens centred round an old cartwheel. Sadly these usually rot after a year or two but can look most effective while they last. Many herbs can withstand quite rough treatment, and a path including various kinds of thyme can make a fragrant feature for garden visitors to savour as they stroll until the thyme expires. In a formal layout, the use of paving slabs can help keep these often rampaging plants under some semblance of control. It is also easier to reach the herbs when popping out from the house in slippers!

Many herbs can be grown with no garden at all. A hanging basket filled with herbs can make an attractive and scented feature outside the kitchen door, and even tolerates the inevitable neglect which so often happens with us. There are also pleasing stacking pots of terracotta for planting with an assortment of herbs to suit the cook in charge.

The choice of plants is a wide one, and any list should begin with those herbs the grower is really sure of using and will not let go all straggly. Those described below will all do well in Kent if raised in the right conditions.

Chives
This decorative plant has a milder flavour than onions, and its tufts of tubular leaves are topped by attractive rosy flowers in early summer. It prefers a moist soil rich in humus, and should be grown in a sunny position. Overcrowded clumps should be lifted and divided every few years in autumn or spring, and the plant can also be grown from seed. In recent years a form described as Garlic

Chives has appeared. Chopped leaves are sprinkled over most savoury dishes and added to soups, omelettes and salads.

Fennel

Worth growing for its feathery foliage alone, this attractive herb has an acquired taste of aniseed. Although a perennial, the flavour is better in younger parts of the plant. Older plants are usually divided in winter and replanted, or further stock grown from seed or the tiny seedlings found growing around the parent plant. Mainly used with fish such as herrings and mackerel.

Garlic

By no means a universal favourite but gaining in popularity, this strong-flavoured herb is easily grown in Kent. The bulbs are divided into their segments or 'cloves' which are planted in much the same way as onion sets in a sheltered, sunny position. The flowering stem should be removed, and the bulbs lifted in August when the foliage starts turning yellow. Leave to ripen in the sunshine, and store in a string like onions in a dry, warm place.

Horseradish

A herb to be planted with caution as it can be invasive and once well established will go on from year to year. Its dock-like leaves are far from attractive, but the grated root is unequalled as an accompaniment to roast beef when made into a sauce with vinegar and cream.

Marjoram

There are three types of this herb: pot, sweet and wild marjoram (oregano). Pot marjoram is the easiest to grow, but has less flavour. Treat sweet marjoram as a half hardy annual grown from seed. Oregano is the most strongly flavoured and should be used with discretion. Meat, egg and fish dishes are all enhanced by this herb which dries well for preserving if cut as the flower buds are starting to open. It should be dried in bunches in a warm, airy, sunless place and also freezes well.

Mint

A universal favourite which has many forms, including common mint (spearmint), apple mint, eau de Cologne mint, ginger mint, peppermint, and pineapple mint. Mint spreads rapidly, and is best confined by planting in a bottomless bucket buried in the ground. It prefers damp soil and is sometimes affected by rust. If signs of orange patches are seen, the infected plants should be pulled up and destroyed. A few rooted stems potted up in late summer and grown on a windowsill will provide a supply of fresh mint through the winter.

Rosemary

A hardy evergreen shrub growing to about four feet high, its fragrant leaves have a distinctive flavour. If sprigs are placed around roasting meats such as lamb the flavour will be much enhanced. It thrives in a well-drained, sheltered and sunny position and is easily propagated by cuttings taken in early spring, and rooted in pots of peat and sharp sand. Prune regularly early in the year to prevent a straggly appearance.

Sage

A most versatile, evergreen shrub which is generally hardy in all but the coldest of winters. Occurs in several forms but those most used for cooking are the broad leaved and narrow leaved sages. The chopped leaves can be sprinkled over dishes and used in stuffing the stronger flavoured meats. Sage grows best on a rich but light ground in a sunny position and is happy on our chalky Kentish soil. The plants become straggly after a few years and are best replaced by cuttings, layering or dividing the old plant.

Tarragon

A pungent herb with two forms, French and Russian, each having a characteristic flavour of their own; French tarragon is sometimes called the King of Herbs, and this is the one to grow. Its chopped leaves can be added to chicken dishes and salads. Tarragon vinegar is made by leaving young shoots in wine vinegar for two weeks. It grows to around three feet and does best in a sunny spot in a humus-rich but well-drained soil. Best divided every four years and replanted to avoid it becoming overcrowded. Propagated by shoots with a portion of root attached.

Thyme

Although more than sixty species of thyme are known, only two kinds are mainly used as culinary herbs: these are Garden thyme (Thymus vulgaris) and Lemon thyme (T. citriodorus). These hardy, dwarf evergreen shrubs are easy to grow from seeds sown in spring or from cuttings rooted in April and May. The shoots can be used fresh or may be dried or frozen before the plants have flowered. Grow in a sunny, well-drained position and replace every few years before they become too straggly. Lemon thyme is less hardy than Garden thyme, but is attractive to bees and gives their honey a delicious flavour.

Some herbs to grow from seed each year:

Sweet Basil
A half hardy annual which grows to a height of 2 – 3 feet. Its pale green leaves have a clove-like flavour, and are used sparingly in curries and similar dishes. Cooked tomatoes are also enhanced by this herb which has several forms including the decorative purple basil. Sow seeds in their growing position in early May, and thin the seedlings to a foot apart.

Borage
A hardy annual which can reach a height of 3 feet. Its refreshing, cucumber-like flavour is used in drinks and salads, and the attractive blue flowers can be candied for cake decoration. It thrives in almost any kind of soil as long as the spot is a sunny one.

Dill
Similar in appearance to fennel, this hardy annual can be sown in its growing position in April, followed by successive sowings until June if a supply of leaves is required. Prefers a sunny, sheltered border which should be kept well weeded to give the seedlings a chance to grow. The seeds can be used in salads or with fish, and the finely chopped leaves also add flavour to fish dishes. Seeds scatter easily, so this herb is best gathered as soon as the flowers become brown, pulling up the plants or cutting at ground level.

Parsley
A universal favourite, this biennial is best grown fresh from seed each year as the young plants have a rather better flavour. Germination can be slow, but hot water in the drills before sowing from April speeds up the process. Fertile, well-drained soil is best and the plants prefer partial shade. Parsley can also be grown in pots and other containers and looks most decorative. Rich in vitamins and minerals, this useful herb is an attractive garnish, and fine for sauces and stuffing.

Chapter Twenty One

Success with Shrubs

In recent years, the prospect of lower maintenance offered by many garden shrubs has made them very popular with many busy gardeners. Carefully chosen, a selection of these can offer interest and colour throughout the year.

When planning the planting of shrubs, take careful note of their final sizes, and either leave room for them to grow, or be prepared to move some later on.

Points on planting

Container-grown shrubs can be planted at almost any time of year, providing the ground is not frozen or waterlogged, but the best time to do it is in early autumn. The warmer soil will encourage growth of roots and ensure the shrubs are established before the rigours of winter begin.

To give the shrub the best possible start in life, dig out a generously wide planting hole (but not too deep), and make a planting mixture by adding to the soil removed a similar amount of peat. Then add a good handful of bonemeal to each bucketful of the planting mix. Fork over the base of the hole and work in some of the mixture, together with a sprinkling of general fertilizer. Place the shrub in its hole and adjust the planting mix level so the original planting depth is maintained. Remove the container, and fill in with more of the mix, carefully firming as filling proceeds, and finishing with a slight depression to help retain water. Give water after planting and repeat at weekly intervals for a month and more often if the ground stays dry. Bare rooted shrubs should have their branches cut back by about a third after planting.

The following shrubs can all do well in the county of Kent, and may be seen growing in many gardens. The Royal Horticultural Society's garden at Wisley has a wealth of fine labelled specimens of shrubs, and more can be seen at Wakehurst Place in Sussex, the Savill Garden at Windsor, and of course at Kew. Many of the gardens open to the public under the National Gardens Scheme also feature a fine range of shrubs, and the yellow books 'Gardens of England and Wales' and 'Gardens of Kent' give full details.

Evergreens

Berberis (some species): spiny bushes with yellow or orange flowers, sizes range from small to very large.

Ceanothus (some species): blue flowers, grow against south or west-facing wall. 3 – 6 feet.

Choisya: round bush up to 6 feet. Scented white flowers in late spring.

Cotoneaster (some species): many kinds, from prostrate to very large shrubs. Small red berries which are much liked by birds.

Cytisus (Brooms): most have yellow flowers, but also red/gold. Some grow to 7 feet.

Escallonia: 6 feet. Pink, red and white flowers in summer, makes a good hedge. Does well on the Kent coast.

Euonymus: grown for its foliage which is often variegated.

Garrya: fast growing and can reach 9 feet. Has attractive glossy leaves and catkins.

Helianthemum: very low-growing, 6 – 9 inches high. Many colours of flowers in summer.

Hypericum (semi-evergreen): low-growing shrub with bright yellow flowers. Sizes range from 1 – 6 feet.

Lavandula (Lavender) (Evergrey!): favourite fragrant shrub growing to 4 feet. Becomes straggly if not kept clipped after flowering.

Mahonia: glossy, holly-like leaves and scented yellow flowers followed by attractive berries. Up to 6 feet.

Pieris: one for the acid soils only! Young growth is bright red in spring. Bears sprays of white flowers in early summer. About 6 feet.

Pyracantha (Firethorn): mainly seen on walls, but can make a large bush. Yellow or red berries in autumn. Sharp spines make pruning tricky.

Rhododendrons: acid soils only, except in containers. Vast range of types.

Rosemarinus (Rosemary): aromatic shrub with blue flowers. Can grow to 5 feet. Light soils preferred and needs sun.

Santolina (Cotton Lavender): low-growing shrub with silvery grey leaves and yellow flowers. Does best in a sunny spot.

Senecio: silver leaves and grows to 3 feet. Yellow flowers in summer and does well on the coast in a sheltered spot.

Skimmia: neat, shiny leaves and attractive red berries if both male and female forms are grown. 3 feet.

Viburnum (some species): several forms including the popular 'Tinus' 6 – 10 feet. Can do well on chalky soil.

Deciduous shrubs

Berberis (some species): spiny bushes with yellow or orange flowers, sizes range from small to very large.

Buddleia (Butterfly Bush): several forms with flowers in purple and white, good on chalk in a sunny spot. 6 feet or more if not pruned.

Caryopteris (Blue Spiraea): clusters of small blue fluffy flowers in autumn. 3 feet. Good on chalk.

Ceanothus (some species): blue flowers. Grow against south or west-facing wall. 3 – 6 feet. Hardier than the evergreen kinds.

Ceratostigma (Hardy Plumbago): blue flowers in late summer/autumn. Leaves turn red in autumn. Does well on chalk. 2 feet.

Chaenomeles (Japonica): attractive, red, pink or white flowers in spring, followed by quince fruit in autumn. 4 – 6 feet.

Chimonanthus (Wintersweet): scented yellow flowers in winter, sunny spot on well-drained soil. 9 feet.

Cornus (Dogwood): attractive coloured bark (!) in winter follows hard pruning. Up to 5 feet.

Cotinus (Smoke Bush): dark red leaves and feathery flowers in June. Full sun on light loam preferred. 5 – 10 feet.

Cotoneaster (some species): many kinds from prostrate to very large shrubs. Small red berries much liked by birds. Red autumn leaves.

Cytisus (Brooms): mostly yellow flowers but also red/gold. Some grow to 7 feet. Do well in poor soils but sometimes short-lived.

Daphne: the pink flowered D. mezereum is most popular kind. Rich soil preferred. 2 – 3 feet.

Deutzia: pink or white flowers in June. Does well in most locations including sun or partial shade. 4 – 6 feet.

Forsythia: universally popular spring-flowering shrub. Yellow flowers followed by bright green foliage. 6 – 8 feet.

Hamamelis (Witch Hazel): attractive, scented winter-flowering shrub, dislikes chalky soil. 10 feet.

Hydrangea: several kinds, with large attractive flowers in late summer. Rich soil in light shade. 5 feet.

Jasminum (Jasmine): winter jasmine has yellow flowers on untidy branches. Any soil, sprawling but cheerful.

Kerria (Jew's Mallow): single or double yellow flowers in late spring. Prefers a sheltered site. Up to 8 feet depending on type.

Kolkwitzia (Beauty Bush): attractive but unscented flowers in May/June. Thrives in chalky soil. 8 feet if unchecked.

Philadelphus (Mock Orange): scented white flowers June/July. Any soil, height 2 – 10 feet depending on variety.

Potentilla (Shrubby Cinquefoil): flowers from May – September in yellow, white or red. Any well-drained soil. Prefers partial shade. 1 – 5 feet.

Rhus (Sumach): large leaves great for autumn colour. Invasive suckers a menace near lawns. 12 + feet.

Ribes (Flowering Currant): pink flowers in spring have cat-like scent. Vigorous shrub happy anywhere. 7 feet.

Sambucus (Elder): golden and variegated-leaved forms are an attractive addition to any garden. 6 feet.

Spiraea: several kinds. Spring flowering are white, summer flowering pink or red. Fertile soil. Sun or partial shade. 2 – 8 feet.

Syringa (Lilac): often grown as a tree, the flowers are white, yellow or rose-purple. Single or double. Happy on chalk. 5 – 12 feet.

Viburnum (some species): several forms including the popular 'Fragrans', 6 – 10 feet. Can do well on chalky soil.

Weigela: attractive trumpet-shaped flowers in pinks and reds. Happy on chalky soil. 4 – 7 feet.

Chapter Twenty Two

A Kentish Gardener's Calendar

January

This is the month for clearing up and planning in the garden — and for taking it easy. Any leaves remaining on the lawn should be raked up and put on the compost heap before heavy snowfalls arrive to cover Kent. Indoors, plan the vegetable garden for the coming season and send off seed orders to avoid disappointment if the seedsmen's stocks run out. If not done over Christmas, be sure to sow some onion seeds in the greenhouse propagator for potting on and planting out in spring. Onion sets planted later may be easier, but for the biggest onions, sow seeds of Kelsae or Robinson's Mammoth. Both do well in our county, and will produce those prize-winning specimens for the local show — and next winter's stews!

Dahlia tubers stored away from frost need checking this month, and any rotting ones thrown out or the affected parts removed and dusted with flowers of sulphur. If storage conditions are too dry, the tubers may be found to be shrivelled. If so, soak them in lukewarm water overnight, and when dry, dust with further flowers of sulphur to keep any fungus at bay. Then return to storage in their boxes of dryish peat — and wash your hands to remove the sulphur smell.

Pruning of fruit trees can be tackled this month on days when frost is absent, and spraying done with tar oil winter wash if not applied last year. Any newly planted fruit trees should be firmed down with the feet if loosened in the ground by frost. The same applies to turf laid in the autumn: check that any turves lifted by earlier frosts are firmed down again, but never when the ground is frozen or the marks will last until spring.

Seed sowing will be some weeks away yet, but if cloches are put out now, the ground will be prewarmed for when the time comes, germination will be faster, and the cat will have somewhere to sleep. Gardens on our heavy Kentish clay can have any remaining vacant ground dug when clear of frost, taking care to leave the surface in largish lumps. As we are always being told, this allows the freezing winter weather to break them down and make it easier to obtain a good tilth at sowing time. Digging on our lighter, sandy soils is best left until the spring.

A greenhouse gives scope for work indoors whatever the weather outside, we always say, and a few minutes each week removing dead

111

or yellowing leaves will improve the plants' appearance and reduce the risk of diseases gaining a hold. If pests are a problem, the house can be fumigated. A combined pest and disease smoke will penetrate the nooks and crannies where overwintering creatures lurk, and avoid the high humidity caused if liquid sprays are used at this time.

That wonderful climber wistaria will flower far better if given its winter pruning this month. Cut back the shoots pruned last summer to two or three buds from their base, and this will encourage flowering spurs to form. Snow will often gather on conifers and other shrubs this month, and needs dislodging with a broom before it accumulates and breaks branches. Pay attention to ponds, too, and clear a patch of ice by melting with a pan of hot water. Never break the ice by hitting, or the shock will kill or injure the fish.

February
Often the coldest month of the year in Kent, but when the ground is free from frost a number of jobs can be done. Jerusalem artichokes have an acquired taste but are easy to grow, and their tall growth can make a useful screen for unsightly sheds and suchlike. Plant them fifteen inches apart and four inches deep. The crop can be left in the ground and lifted as required. Parsnips are often left so that frost can improve their flavour, but if left much longer will start to grow again. Seeds can be sown this month for another crop of this tasty vegetable if the ground is not too wet or frozen, but if delayed for several weeks it will still do well.

Fruit trees will benefit from a high-nitrogen fertilizer this month. Any cankers seen on them should be cut away with a sharp knife and the area treated with a sealing compound to stop diseases getting in. Winter flowering shrubs need pruning as soon as their flowers have faded, and in the rose garden a final clearance of fallen leaves will help reduce the risk of black spot. Slug activity can increase this month, and alpines can usefully be protected with slug pellets under a piece of tile to keep pets and wildlife away.

Towards the end of the month, shallots can be planted nine inches apart in a well-drained, open position, placing further rows a foot apart. Cloves of garlic can also be planted this month, but onion sets are best left until March. Be sure to unpack these as soon as they arrive, and spread in trays in a light, airy, frost-proof place. Stored dahlia tubers can be started into growth in the warm in trays of moist peat to give material for taking cuttings next month.

Kentish cobnuts are far less widespread in the county than once they were, but some lucky gardeners still have them. Prune as soon as the first small red female flowers are seen.

An early sowing of broad beans is worth making late in the month if the ground is right, together with spinach, and turnips. As soon as seed potatoes are purchased, be sure to unpack them and set out, eyes uppermost, in trays to sprout in a light, airy, frost-proof place as for the onion sets. This 'chitting' will help ensure a larger crop of bigger, better potatoes at harvest time.

February is a fine month for overhauling and cleaning any garden tools not oiled and sharpened at the end of last season. Put up proper hooks and racks in the shed if storage arrangements are poor. Garden tools are a valuable asset and will last almost for ever if properly stored and maintained.

March

In gardens with beds and borders of herbaceous perennials, this is the month for lifting and dividing these useful plants to make more room and give extra stock for your fortunate friends with big gardens. Large clumps can be split apart with ease if two forks are inserted back to back. Roots from around the edge of clumps will often do better than those from the centre, and should be replanted as soon as possible after being divided.

Hungry birds can cause much damage to fruit trees by taking the buds: protection given now will help ensure a larger crop in summer. Raspberry canes will benefit greatly from a mulch of rotted manure when the ground is really damp. This not only nourishes the plants but helps retain vital moisture in dry spells, suppresses weeds, and keeps the gardener warm in keen March winds.

In the vegetable garden many sowings can be made this month, but only when the ground is right. Check by walking across the plot: if the soil sticks to your boots the ground is still too wet for sowing. Peas and carrots can be started early in the month, and in mid March the seed potatoes can be set out in rows four inches deep, earthed-up to protect the tender tubers against frost, light and blight. Put in some well rotted compost at the same time and dress the ground with a 2oz Growmore to each square yard between the ridges. Existing spring cabbages can look a trifle woebegone around now, but a dressing of fertilizer lightly worked in around the plants will soon have them colouring up and growing away well.

If sweet pea plants are overwintering in the cold frame, prepare the ground now, if not done earlier, by taking out a trench to a good spade's depth and filling with really good compost or well-rotted farmyard manure, all ready to receive the plants next month. A similar trench for runner beans in the vegetable plot can also be made now and save work later on.

114

In the heated greenhouse, take cuttings from the dahlia tubers started into growth last month, and set them around the edge of pots of 50/50 peat and sharp sand. Stand them in a propagator to give some bottom heat, and move to separate labelled pots when new growth shows that rooting has begun. Tomatoes for growing in the heated greenhouse can be started around the middle of the month. Be sure to transplant the seedlings into 3-inch pots as soon as the first leaves open, and set the plants so these are just clear of the surface. Keep growing on without a check, and leave plenty of room between the pots, to stop them getting straggly on the staging.

Towards the end of March, the sowing of half hardy annuals can be started in the greenhouse propagator to produce the summer bedding plants.

April
As growth of grass gets under way, give the lawn a light mowing if the state of the ground is right. Set the cutter high to avoid scalping and damaging the grass. New lawns can be sown now on ground prepared earlier, using a matchboxful of seed to each square yard and carefully raking into the levelled surface. Protect with netting against birds, or use polythene sheet on small areas. Be sure to remove this as soon as the young grass appears.

Sweet pea plants from an October sowing which have overwintered in the cold frame can be set out now beside 8-ft canes, along ground prepared beforehand (see March). These should have several shoots attached and, a few weeks after planting, the best one should be selected for training up the cane, and the others removed.

Tomato plants can be set out now in the frost-free greenhouse for growing in large pots, peat-filled growing bags or by ring culture. Delay planting until the first yellow flowers have opened, and start feeding only when the first tiny fruits have set. It pays to wait.

In the vegetable garden, onion sets can be planted now, at six-inch spacing in rows a foot apart. Set them so the tips are just below the surface, and if possible place galvanized wire netting pea guards over the rows to prevent them being tweaked from the ground by birds. Remove the guards as soon as the onion leaves begin to grow through them.

In mid April well-hardened violas and pansies can be planted, and sowings of hardy annual seeds made in their flowering positions in open ground. This can be rather chancy in some seasons, though, and they are better raised under cover in the same way as bedding plants if facilities for this are available.

The main sowings of vegetable seeds are usually made towards the middle of this month in Kent, but always be prepared to delay the work if damp and cold conditions persist. In addition to the usual vegetable seeds, remember to make a sowing of parsley along the edge of a paved path where this useful crop can find hidden reserves of moisture in dry spells.

Bedding plants raised from seed and pricked out into trays, should now be hardening off in the cold frame. Close the frame at night if frost threatens, but give full ventilation in the daytime, and water regularly.

May

The month of Chelsea's great flower show, and few frosts occur in Kent once the second week has passed. Even before this, the dahlia tubers saved from last year can be planted in the ground, but any plants raised from cuttings should wait until the month's third week.

Diseases of roses are more widespread since the Clean Air Act removed sulphur fumes and suchlike, and regular spraying against black spot, mildew and rust, as well as pests, should become routine from now on. Ring the changes between various brands of insecticide/fungicide formulations, follow the makers' instructions, and spray in the evening to avoid killing bees and other beneficial insects.

Tomatoes can now be planted in unheated greenhouses, as long as the door and ventilators are firmly shut at night while any chance of frost remains (see April). As the sun's power increases, apply shading to the greenhouse roof to reduce risk of scorching and greenback as the fruits ripen. Feed with a high potash liquid fertilizer and remove the side shoots as they appear.

Growth should be rapid on the vegetable plot by now, and thinning must be done without delay to prevent overcrowded plants and spoilt crops. Thin out carrots, parsnip, beet and onion seedlings in two stages: to three inches at first and six after a week or two. Most of these second stage thinnings are large enough for salads or pickling, but when pulling them out be sure to firm down the disturbed soil to lessen the chances of pest attacks. Chinese cabbage are becoming popular for salads, and can be sown now where they are to grow. Avoid transplanting this crop as they will almost certainly 'bolt' and be wasted. Continue to earth up potatoes as they grow. Towards the end of the month, ridge cucumbers and marrows can be planted out on ridges or mounds in well-manured ground, and kept watered.

When cutting the first asparagus shoots, they are often few and far between, but can be stored for a while in the fridge until a usable quantity has accrued. If their cutting is delayed they will be too far gone by the time the others are ready.

By mid May the runner beans started earlier under glass can be planted outside, to grow up sticks, strings or canes. Keep the roots well watered as they grow, and this will encourage better setting of the first flowers and earlier pickings of this favourite garden vegetable.

Strawberries crop well in the county of Kent, and a layer of straw should be placed under the plants this month to protect the ripening fruits from mud splashed up in rainy spells. Under this, a light sprinkling of slug pellets will help prevent these pests attacking the fruit. A simple net arranged on wire hoops along the row will stop any damage by birds.

Lawn weeds become a problem this month but are easily controlled with selective weedkillers, as long as they are in active growth. Avoid drift on to nearby plants, and keep pets or children off the grass until the liquid has dried.

Most of the summer bedding plants can be set out in mid May, and if space is still occupied by last spring's bulbs, these can be lifted and replanted in spare ground to finish building up next year's flowers before the leaves die down. Set the bedding plants firmly in the ground, and water well, followed by a weekly liquid feed as they become established. Hanging baskets can also go out at this time, taking care to give regular water and feeds to prevent them drying out and to encourage vigorous growth. Also plant out window boxes this month, but ensure they are strongly fixed.

June

The month when many rewards are reaped for our gardening labours. The first new potatoes may be ready, but lift only as required and leave the rest to go on growing in the ground for a while. Later-planted potatoes should still be earthed up to stop summer rains washing away the soil and letting in light. This will turn the tubers green and poisonous.

Outdoor tomatoes should be planted this month, preferably in a sunny but sheltered spot. With modern, specially bred varieties, this crop is far less of a gamble than once it was. 'Red Alert' has small tomatoes, but in a good year can be fruiting ahead of plants in some greenhouses. If this or other bush varieties are grown, be sure to put down straw or black polythene beneath the plants, and sprinkle some slug pellets underneath.

Cease cutting asparagus by the end of the month and allow the remaining shoots to grow. These need tying to canes to keep them upright and nourish the crowns for next year's crop. In October, when they have yellowed, the ferny growths are cut down to ground level and cleared away. A further sowing of French beans can be made outside this month for a useful late crop, and a sowing of parsley will thrive while the soil is warm and moist. Continue to thin vegetable seedlings before overcrowding occurs. Lift autumn-sown onions by the end of this month, to bridge the gap between last year's stored onions and the new main crop.

As the new raspberry canes grow up, they should be spaced out and tied in with string to supporting wires. Clusters of apples will normally be thinned by the 'June drop' (which happens mainly in July), but it is useful now to go round and remove any mis-shapen ones, lest they grow at the expense of better fruit. Put netting round soft fruits such as currants and gooseberries to keep the birds away.

Even the most tender bedding plants can be set out this month. Remember that dahlias are gross feeders, and if the ground was not manured beforehand, be sure to give regular liquid feeds as the plants develop. Mottled leaves are a sign of virus in the plants, and any so affected should be taken up and discarded.

Aubrietias finish flowering this month, and should then be trimmed back with scissors to keep them compact. Overcrowded clumps of irises need lifting and dividing, and the spraying of roses with fungicide should continue.

In the greenhouse, keep a careful watch for pests and diseases, and fumigate overnight if needed. Sow calceolarias in well-drained compost for a colourful show later, and pot up May-sown cinerarias before having a much needed rest. Finish the potting-on of perpetual flowering carnations grown from cuttings, and continue feeding greenhouse tomatoes at every watering. If yellow mottling is seen between veins on their leaves, drench with solution of Epsom Salts to correct the magnesium deficiency.

July

To keep the Kentish garden full of flowers throughout high summer, regular removal of dead or faded blooms is vital. If plants are allowed to set seed the flowers will cease. Feeding and watering must continue this month, especially with patio pots, hanging baskets and window boxes.

In the vegetable garden, spray the maincrop potatoes with Bordeaux mixture to protect against blight, and treat tomatoes at the same time. Runner beans will benefit from a mulch of garden compost after rain, and should be picked every few days to keep further beans coming. Spring greens, spinach and turnips can be sown this month, together with more Chinese cabbage. Earlier sowings of these should be thinned out. Earth up rows of early celery to ensure good blanching, and 'stop' outdoor tomatoes by pinching out the tips when four fruit trusses have formed.

Where extra strawberry plants are required to extend the bed, peg down some runners to take root, but be sure the parent plants are healthy. Cut off and burn any plum branches showing signs of silver leaf disease, and later this month pick any apples that part readily from the branches when handled. Cut out raspberry canes that have finished fruiting.

The first pruning of wistaria should be done this month: shorten any long growths to six inches from their base, except where needed to extend the coverage or fill in gaps. Further pruning will be needed in the winter (see January) to keep this splendid climber flowering well each year.

Gather herbs for storage, and hang in small bunches to dry in a cool, dark place. Store in paper bags or dark glass jars and label to ensure they are not kept too long.

Check any holiday plans to keep the greenhouse and other indoor plants growing well, and be sure the arrangements are working before you depart. Capillary matting is useful on greenhouse staging, but many pot plants can be plunged in the soil in a shady place outside, and watered well before departing.

August

The garden generally assumes a slower pace this month, thank goodness, and there is more time to enjoy it, sitting in the shade or busy round the barbecue. But the cutting of hedges should be finished soon, taking care to achieve a wider base sloping inwards towards the top. Cut the sides first and this will let trimmings from the top fall easily to the ground to be collected.

Cuttings of geraniums (pelargoniums) taken this month for the greenhouse will be rooted in time for winter storage in the minimum of space, and hydrangea cuttings can be put to root now in single pots in a shady place outside. Freesia corms should be planted six to a 5-inch pot, left in the cold frame and kept watered until being brought into the heated greenhouse when autumn frosts threaten.

In the vegetable garden, some stump-rooted carrots can be sown now in a sheltered place, and early beetroot lifted for pickling. Later in the month, make a sowing of spinach beet and winter spinach (if you like it), and sow some Japanese onions. These will stand over winter to give a useful gap-filling crop early next summer, and some handy salad onions when the plants are thinned out. As this year's main crop onions reach their final size, some gardeners favour bending over the leaves to assist ripening. Modern practice doubts this does much good, but the rows look very much tidier as a result!

Continue to feed greenhouse tomatoes with a high potash fertilizer, and pinch out the growing tips when they reach the roof. Any withered lower leaves are best removed now to allow good circulation of air and lessen the risk of grey mould or botrytis gaining a hold.

September

Where cabbage white butterflies have been active, a spray with Picket will kill off any caterpillars and leave the crop ready for harvest next day if needed. At the same time, remove dead leaves from any of the brassicas, and plant out spring cabbages to stand through the winter. Maincrop carrots and potatoes can be lifted now for storage in paper sacks once they have dried, and any remaining outdoor tomatoes and the rest of the runner beans gathered before the month ends.

Planting of bulbs for spring flowering can be started now and continued next month as more space becomes available. Meanwhile, regular removal of dead and faded blooms in pots and other containers will prolong the summer's display for a few more weeks.

In some places a sowing of hardy annuals can be made outside, and tender plants such as bedding geraniums lifted for safe storage through the winter. Late-flowering chrysanthemums should be moved to the greenhouse by the end of the month.

Ill-drained lawns should be aerated this month by spiking with a fork or hollow-tined aerator to assist drainage through the winter, and scarifying done with a wire rake to remove the dead grasses or 'thatch' which built up through the summer. If any feeding is needed, be sure to use a special low nitrogen, autumn food, or lush grasses may result and encourage disease as well as unwelcome extra mowing.

Soft new growth sometimes follows the summer pruning of fruit trees and this should be nipped off before the season ends.

October

Sweet peas can be sown at several times of year, but the best results are gained by sowing in October and overwintering these hardy plants in the frame before planting out next spring. Sow in the greenhouse in 3-inch pots or special fibre sweet pea tubes of a loam-based compost, pinch out the tops when four pairs of leaves have formed, and move to the cold frame.

Garden ponds repay an autumn clean-up, and the job should start with thinning out the oxygenating plants and removing old water lily leaves. Put all material removed in a bucket first, and examine to ensure that small fish and other creatures are not thrown away with the rubbish.

Any remaining apples and pears should be gathered this month as they become ready, and sites for planting new fruit trees and bushes prepared by digging, removing all perennial weeds and working in some well-rotted manure.

Mint can be hard to find in the winter months, but if a few roots are potted up now in some damp compost and placed in the greenhouse or even on a windowsill indoors, a supply will be available for cutting as required.

In the vegetable garden, sow some lettuces for growing under cloches, and earth up late celery. Turnips should be lifted now and stored in a frost-free place, and a row of broad beans sown outside in a sheltered place. For these autumn sowings the variety Aquadulce is one of the best. Digging of vacant ground on heavy, clay soils can be continued.

Autumn is acknowledged to be 'nature's time for planting' and deciduous trees and shrubs put in now will have time for their roots to become better established before the winter sets in. Gladioli corms can be lifted now and stored, and tulips planted in their spring flowering positions, as well as wallflowers and pansies. Clear the fallen leaves before they accumulate in rock gardens and pools. In the greenhouse, finish any potting-on still to be done and fumigate at night if pests are a problem.

November

Overhaul the lawn mower this month and send away if necessary. Most gardens have masses of fallen leaves on the lawn and they can either be put on the compost heap, or used to make excellent leafmould for mulching. If a simple enclosure of wire netting is made with a post at each corner, the leaves will rot down to a fraction of the space first filled. Some leaves such as horse chestnut take much longer to decompose but will do so in the end and are still better used than burnt.

Early in the month a row of hardy peas can be sown for an early crop next year, and Jerusalem artichokes lifted as required for use. Forcing of rhubarb can be started by digging up a few crowns to become frosted. They can later be moved to light-tight boxes in the greenhouse or cellar.

Ventilate the greenhouse with care from now on, and check any heating arrangements to be sure they are functioning well. Pots of bulbs in plunge beds can be brought inside this month when their required spell in cold and dark has been served, but move them to a cool place first.

December

Many stored apples can be eaten with relish this month, and these should be examined at intervals. Remove any rotting ones before the trouble spreads, and consume the disfigured ones first. Any stored vegetables should also be checked in the same way.

Ponds may well be frozen for part of this month and a patch can be kept clear by floating a plastic ball or inflated inner tube on the surface. This will allow the fish to breathe, and harmful gases to escape.

There is plenty of scope for exercise in most gardens after any excess at Christmas! Badly drained lawns can be spiked with a fork unless they are frosty, and vacant heavy ground dug over and left rough. For something less strenuous, sow some onion seeds in the greenhouse propagator, and prepare the seed list for next year. Happy Christmas!

Appendix

Some Useful Books for Further Reading

'A – Z of Garden Pests and Problems'. Ian G. Walls. Collins.
'Clematis'. Christopher Lloyd. Collins.
'Directory of Garden Chemicals'. British Agrochemicals Association.
'Encyclopaedia of Garden Plants and Flowers'. Reader's Digest, 1976.
The 'Expert' series of books by Dr D.G. Hessayon. PBI.
'The Fruit Garden Displayed'. Royal Horticultural Society.
The 'Garden' series leaflets on fruit. East Malling IHR.
'Gardening Month by Month'. Patrick Johns. Collingridge.
'Gardens of England and Wales'. National Gardens Scheme.
'Greenhouse Gardening'. Sue Phillips. Hamlyn.
'Growing Herbs'. Rosemary Titterington. Crowood Press.
'How to Grow and Use Herbs'. Ann Bonar & Daphne MacCarthy. Ward Lock.
'Illustrated Guide to Gardening'. Reader's Digest.
'The New Small Garden'. C.E. Lucas-Phillips. Collins.
'Notcutts Book of Plants'. Notcutts.
'The Vegetable Garden Displayed'. Royal Horticultural Society & Cassell.
'Your Garden Week by Week'. A.G. Hellyer. Hamlyn.

INDEX

Meresborough Books

17 STATION ROAD, RAINHAM, GILLINGHAM, KENT. ME8 7RS

Telephone Medway (0634) 388812

We are a specialist publisher of books about Kent. Our books are available in most bookshops in the county, including our own at this address. Alternatively you may order direct, adding 10% for post (minimum 20p, orders over £20 post free). ISBN prefix 0 905270 for 3 figure numbers, 094819 for 4 figure numbers. Titles in print November 1989.

BYGONE KENT. A monthly journal on all aspects of Kent history founded October 1979. £1.50 per month. Annual Subscription £16.50. All back numbers available (some in photocopy).

HARDBACKS

AIRCRAFT CASUALTIES IN KENT Part One 1939-40 compiled by G.G. Baxter, K.A. Owen and P. Baldock. ISBN 3506. £10.95.

BARGEBUILDING ON THE SWALE by Don Sattin. ISBN 3530. £10.95.

EDWARDIAN CHISLEHURST by Arthur Battle. ISBN 3433. £9.95.

FISHERMEN FROM THE KENTISH SHORE by Derek Coombe. ISBN 3409. £10.95.

THE GILLS by Tony Conway. ISBN 266. £5.95. **BARGAIN OFFER £1.95.**

JUST OFF THE SWALE by Don Sattin. ISBN 045. £5.95.

KENT CASTLES by John Guy. ISBN 150. £7.50.

KENT'S OWN by Robin J. Brooks. The history of 500 (County of Kent) Squadron of the R.A.A.F. ISBN 541. £5.95.

LIFE AND TIMES OF THE EAST KENT CRITIC by Derrick Molock. ISBN 3077. **BARGAIN OFFER £1.95.**

THE LONDON, CHATHAM & DOVER RAILWAY by Adrian Gray. ISBN 886. £7.95.

THE NATURAL HISTORY OF ROMNEY MARSH by Dr F.M. Firth, M.A., Ph.D. ISBN 789. £6.95.

A NEW DICTIONARY OF KENT DIALECT by Alan Major. ISBN 274. £7.50.

O FAMOUS KENT by Eric Swain. ISBN 738. £9.95. **BARGAIN OFFER £4.95.**

THE PAST GLORY OF MILTON CREEK by Alan Cordell and Leslie Williams. ISBN 3042. £9.95.

ROCHESTER FROM OLD PHOTOGRAPHS compiled by the City of Rochester Society. Large format. ISBN 975. £7.95. (Also available in paperback ISBN 983. £4.95.)

SHERLOCK HOLMES AND THE KENT RAILWAYS by Kelvin Jones. ISBN 3255. £8.95.

SOUTH EAST BRITAIN: ETERNAL BATTLEGROUND by Gregory Blaxland. A military history. ISBN 444. £5.95.

STRATFORD HOUSE SCHOOL 1912-1987 by Susan Pittman. ISBN 3212. £10.00.

TALES OF VICTORIAN HEADCORN or The Oddities of Heddington by Penelope Rivers (Ellen M. Poole). ISBN 3050. £8.95. (Also available in paperback ISBN 3069. £3.95.)

TEYNHAM MANOR AND HUNDRED (798-1935) by Elizabeth Selby, MBE. ISBN 630. £5.95.

TROOPSHIP TO CALAIS by Derek Spiers. ISBN 3395. £11.95.

TWO HALVES OF A LIFE by Doctor Kary Pole. ISBN 509. £5.95.

US BARGEMEN by A.S. Bennett. ISBN 207. £6.95.

A VIEW OF CHRIST'S COLLEGE, BLACKHEATH by A.E.O. Crombie, B.A. ISBN 223. £6.95.

LARGE FORMAT PICTORIAL PAPERBACKS

ARE YOU BEING SERVED, MADAM? by Molly Proctor. ISBN 3174. £3.50.
AVIATION IN KENT by Robin J. Brooks. ISBN 681. £2.95.
BEFORE AND AFTER THE HURRICANE IN AND AROUND CANTERBURY by Paul Crampton. ISBN 3387. £3.50.
THE BLITZ OF CANTERBURY by Paul Crampton. ISBN 3441. £3.50.
EAST KENT FROM THE AIR by John Guy. ISBN 3158. £3.50.
EAST SUSSEX RAILWAYS IN OLD POSTCARDS by Kevin Robertson. ISBN 3220. £3.50.
GEORGE BARGEBRICK Esq. by Richard-Hugh Perks. ISBN 479. £4.50.
HEADCORN: A Pictorial History by the Headcorn Local History Society. ISBN 3271. £3.50.
KENT TOWN CRAFTS by Richard Filmer. ISBN 584. £2.95.
THE LIFE AND ART OF ONE MAN by Dudley Pout. ISBN 525. £2.95.
THE MEDWAY TOWNS FROM THE AIR by Piers Morgan and Diane Nicholls. ISBN 3557. £4.95.
MORE PICTURES OF RAINHAM by Barbara Mackay Miller. ISBN 3298. £3.50.
THE MOTOR BUS SERVICES OF KENT AND EAST SUSSEX — A brief history by Eric Baldock. ISBN 959. £4.95.
OLD BROADSTAIRS by Michael David Mirams. ISBN 3115. £3.50.
OLD CHATHAM: A THIRD PICTURE BOOK by Philip MacDougall. ISBN 3190. £3.50.
OLD FAVERSHAM by Arthur Percival. ISBN 3425. £3.50.
OLD GILLINGHAM by Philip MacDougall. ISBN 3328. £3.50.
OLD MAIDSTONE'S PUBLIC HOUSES by Irene Hales. ISBN 533. £2.95.
OLD MAIDSTONE Vol.2 by Irene Hales. ISBN 38X. £2.50.
OLD MAIDSTONE Vol.3 by Irene Hales. ISBN 3336. £3.50.
OLD MARGATE by Michael David Mirams. ISBN 851. £3.50.
OLD PUBS OF TUNBRIDGE WELLS & DISTRICT by Keith Hetherington and Alun Griffiths. ISBN 300X. £3.50.
OLD SANDWICH by Julian Arnold and Andrew Aubertin. ISBN 673. £2.95.
OLD TONBRIDGE by Don Skinner. ISBN 398. £2.50.
PEMBURY IN THE PAST by Mary Standen. ISBN 916. £2.95.
A PICTORIAL STUDY OF ALKHAM PARISH by Susan Lees and Roy Humphreys. ISBN 3034. £2.95.
A PICTORIAL STUDY OF HAWKINGE PARISH by Roy Humphreys. ISBN 328X. £3.50.
A PICTUREBOOK OF OLD RAINHAM by Barbara Mackay Miller. ISBN 606. £3.50.
REMINISCENCES OF OLD CRANBROOK by Joe Woodcock. ISBN 331X. £3.50.
ROCHESTER FROM OLD PHOTOGRAPHS — see under hardbacks.
SMARDEN: A Pictorial History by Jenni Rodger. ISBN 592. £3.50.
THOMAS SIDNEY COOPER OF CANTERBURY by Brian Stewart. ISBN 762. £2.95.
WEST KENT FROM THE AIR by John Guy. ISBN 3166. £3.50.

STANDARD SIZE PAPERBACKS

BIRDS OF KENT: A Review of their Status and Distribution by the Kent Ornithological Society. ISBN 800. £6.95.
BIRDWATCHING IN KENT by Don Taylor. ISBN 932. £4.50.
THE CANTERBURY MONSTERS by J.H. Vaux. ISBN 3468. £2.50.